COOKING FROM MAINLAND CHINA

158 Authentic Recipes from The People's Republic of China

BARRON'S

First U.S. Edition 1979 by
Barron's Educational Series, Inc.

© Copyright 1979 by Sumi Hatano

All rights reserved.
No part of this book may be reproduced
in any form, by photostat, microfilm, xerography,
or any other means, or incorporated into any
information retrieval system, electronic or
mechanical, without the written permission
of the copyright owner.

All inquiries should be addressed to:
Barron's Educational Series, Inc.
113 Crossways Park Drive
Woodbury, New York 11797

Original Edition published by
Shufunotomo Co., Ltd.
1-chome Surugadai, Kanda, Chiyoda-ku,
Tokyo, Japan

Library of Congress Catalog Card No. 79–54702

International Standard Book No. 0–8120–5375–3

PRINTED IN JAPAN

Preface

The Chinese are said to be gourmet cooks of the East. This cookbook will give you an insight into genuine Chinese cuisine and teach you how Chinese dishes are varied, delicious, nutritious, and easy to prepare. A best seller in Mainland China, this book will easily turn both experienced and not-so-experienced Western cooks into specialists in Chinese cooking.

The Masses Cookbook

Introduction

I have been practicing and teaching Chinese cooking for many years, but this is my first time to introduce a large number of dishes by translating them directly from a Chinese cookbook that does not have a single picture.

To express my impression of the book in a few words, it teaches a lot of simple and popular home cooking and shows the roots of Chinese cuisine. Especially deserving of notice are vegetable dishes made of very common and seasonal vegetables in an easy-to-follow method, bringing out the natural flavors and by using ingredients at hand.

If those Chinese vegetable dishes are added to our own repertoire, the variety and nutritional blance of our diet will be greatly improved.

The author of the original book has gathered and introduced simple local dishes handed down from generation to generation. Therefore the Chinese volume is quite different from one dish to another;some dishes serve only one person and the quantity of others is enough for an army. In my present translation the recipes are adjusted to everday standard.

Though the recipes are from all over China, most of them are from northern districts. Therefore most of the dishes are salty and dark colored (due to the Northerner's preference for soy sauce and brown bean paste), rather than flavored with ketchup or cream sauce as is common in Southern districts.

China is so huge a country that the inland people can't get salt water products and have to use *ts'ao-yü* 草魚 *kuei-yü* 桂魚 and carp. These river fish, however, are interchangable with white meat fish by easy-to-follow methods.

I try to avoid changes as much as I could, in order to preserve the original flavor of this deserving cookbook, but in some cases I found the amount of sugar or salt excessive. Whenever I revised the recipe on the basis of my own judgement, I have so indicated in footnotes.

The dishes in this book are very simple and different from the elaborate ones I learned from Chinese cooks in Hongkong. They changed my impression that Chinese cuisine is a complete art and at the same time I was forced to reconsider the history and background of Chinese cuisine.

No culture was created instantly, neither can the art of cooking exist without its accumulation of experiences from the past. This book imparts with its colorful Chinese cooking a sense of the origins of this cooking therefore of the past.

I sincerely hope this book will help you understand China and that it will open a channel of communication through the introduction of China's culinary art.

Sumi Hatano

Contents

How to Prepare Ingredients

Cutting the ingredients in uniform sizes for use in the same dish is extremely important of Chinese cooking. Not just for aesthetic purposes but also for even cooking. For stir-frying, meat is usually sliced or slivered; for long simmering cut into chunks or cubes. One can easily estimate the time needed to cook a dish by the way the ingredients are cut. The names of most Chinese dishes often carry a word indicating just how the ingredients of a given dish are cut.

For example, in "The Masses Cookbook" the character *ssŭ* was used in the dish "Jou-ssŭ-ch'ao-ts'ung-t'ou" 肉絲炒葱頭 hence the dominant ingredient of that dish was in thin slivers, and the word *p'ien* in the dish "Ch'ao-jou-p'ien" 炒肉片 means "thin slice" so one knows immediately the dish was cooked with ingredients thinly sliced.

Here are a few cutting terms used in "The Masses Cookbook."

末 *mo* mince or grind

絲 *ssŭ* sliver

片 *p'ien* slice thinly

丁 *ting* dice

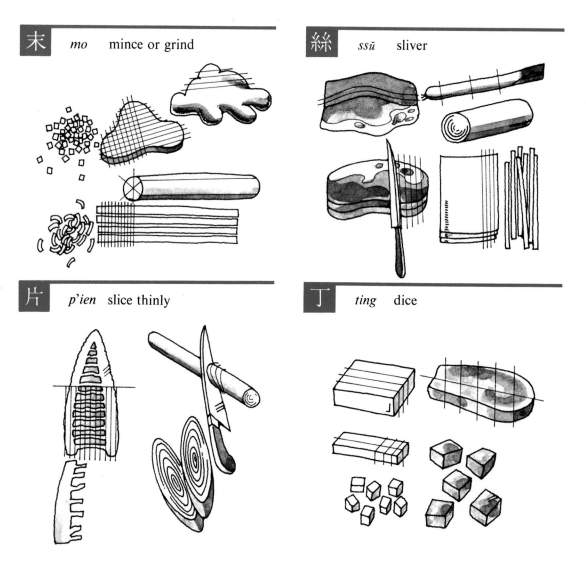

t'iao cut into strips

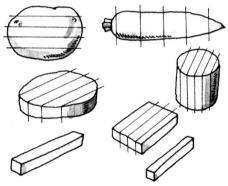

 k'uai cube or cut into chunks

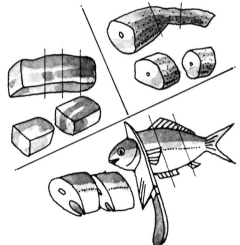

 tuan cut into sections

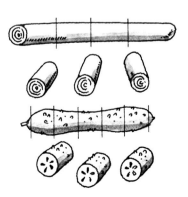

Chinese Ingredients

Information and Suggestions on Some Chinese Ingredients in "The Masses Cookbook"

Cha-ts'ai 搾菜 (Szechuan preserved vegetable)

A lump-like or knob-like preserved vegetable, which is very salty and spicy. A special product of Szechuan. It is coated with chili pepper. Rinse or soak in water for a milder taste. *Cha-ts'ai* may be sliced and served as is, or stir-fried with meat, or cooked in soup with bean curd.

Fên-p'i 粉皮 (Mung bean sheet noodles)

Transparent thin noodle sheets, made from mung bean flour the same as cellophane noodles. They come in 2 inch (6 cm) or 1½ inches (4.5 cm) wide. When using dried ones, boil them in water until soft and let soak in cold water till ready for use. Serve *fên-p'i* with boiled pork or steamed chicken accompanied by a sauce.

Fên-ssŭ 粉絲 (Mung bean noodles)

Fine transparent noodles made from green mung bean *lü-tou* 緑豆. The Japanese type is made from potato starch and when boiled in water the noodles become mushy. The Chinese mung bean noodles stay firm and shiny in boiling water. Must be soaked or parboiled before using. After soaking cut into various lengths and add to dishes that required them.

Fu-i 腐衣 (Bean curd sheets)

A soy bean product, also called *tou-fu-i* 豆腐衣, *fu-i* 腐衣, *tou-chin* 豆筋, or *fu-chu* 腐竹, depending on the shape they are sold in. Bean curd sheets are made in the same process as bean curd. First grind soaked soy beans into a white liquid, then boil the soy milk over a fire. When a thin film is formed on the surface, it is picked up with a pair of bamboo chopsticks, and dried. Fresh *fu-i* can be deep-fried and served with sweet-and-sour sauce; or wrapped with ground meat and deep-fried. When dried bean curd sheets are used, first soak in lukewarm water, then cook with other ingredients.

Szechuan preserved vegetable
(*cha-ts'ai*)

Mung bean noodles
(*fên-ssŭ*)

Bean curd sheets
(*fu-i*)

Dried shrimp
(*hsia-mi*)

Hsia-mi 蝦 米 (Dried shrimp)

Also called "hsai-kan 蝦乾", or "hai-mi 海 米", or "k'ai-yang 開 洋." These have a delicate taste and are used to enrich and flavor dishes much as dried bonito is used in Japanese cooking. Should be rinsed and soaked in lukewarm water before using, reserving the soaking water for soup stock. Dried shrimp usually flavors soups and dishes that are cooked with ingredients such as giant white radish which has a subtle taste.

Hsien-tan 咸 蛋 (Salted eggs)

Duck eggs soaked in a mixture of lye, Chinese rice wine, salt and water. They are sold with a coating of mud and look like black mud balls. The yoks are bright orange and have a very rich taste. One must remove mud before using. Can be hardboiled and served with rice, or used in scrambled eggs.

Hsüeh-ts'ai 雪 菜 (Red-in-snow or pickled mustard greens)

Hsüeh-ts'ai belongs to the rape family. It is a very popular vegetable. It can grow even under the snow and be harvested in the winter when there is no other vegetable available. Soak in water if it is too salty. Can be added to soup or stir-fried with meat.

Kan-sun 干 筍 (Dried bamboo shoots)

This kind of bamboo shoot is preserved by salting, boiling and drying. Should be soaked in water and then boiled for 10 to 15 minutes. Can be substituted for canned bamboo shoots. Will keep for a long time.

Kan-ts'ai 干 菜 (Dried cabbage)

There are many types of kan-ts'ai, it is preserved differently from region to region. Must be soaked and rinsed thoroughly to remove the sand and dirt. In "The Masses Cookbook" it is used to flavor pork stew and soup.

Mi-fên 米 粉 (Rice stick noodles)

Noodles made from rice flour. These are very fine and with an off white color, looking almost like mung bean noodles but not quite as white. The taste and the use are different from mung bean noodles. It is a popular ingredient in rice-producing areas, such as Kwangsi 廣 西 and Fukien 福 建 . Can be hardboiled then stir-fried with other ingredients, or cooked with

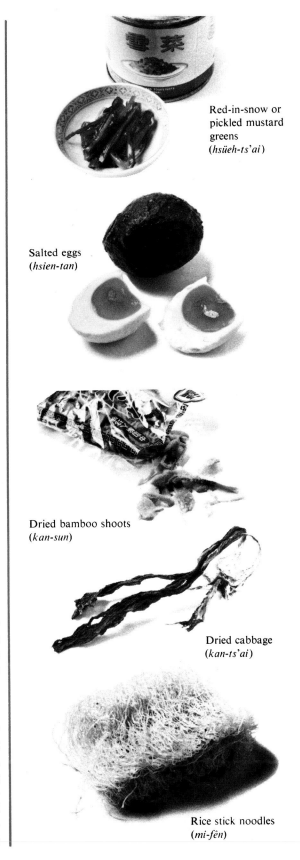

Red-in-snow or pickled mustard greens (hsüeh-ts'ai)

Salted eggs (hsien-tan)

Dried bamboo shoots (kan-sun)

Dried cabbage (kan-ts'ai)

Rice stick noodles (mi-fên)

9

broth and served as soup noodles.

Mu-erh 木耳 (Cloud ears)

A fungus which grows on dead tree bark. When fresh, it is soft and has a crunchy texture. It must be soaked and the woody stems must be removed. Does not have much flavor. Can be added to stir-fried dishes or soup. There is a white kind that is used exclusively for dessert and delicate soups.

Cloud ears
(*mu-erh*)

P'i-tan 皮蛋 (Thousand-year eggs)

P'i-tan are preserved by coating duck eggs with a paste mixture of ashes, salt, tea and rice husks. The black clay coating must be removed before using. The whites have a gelatinous consistency, and the ones speckled with marble-like patterns are considered perfect. Can be sliced into wedges and eaten uncooked as hors d'oeuves, diced and steamed with eggs, or cooked with bean curd.

Thousand-year eggs
(*p'i-tan*)

Seasonings and Spices

Of the many seasonings used in Chinese cooking most are uniquely Chinese. The ability that the Chinese have for blending flavors and combining spices is well matched by their long history and their wisdom. Learn to know the differences between the various seasonings. Practice how and when to use them. Since many of these spices have pronounced flavors and aromas, they should be used sparingly and never allowed to overpower the other ingredients in a dish at the expense of harmony of taste. Star anise and fennel seeds are available in Chinese groceries and drug stores. The list below contains most common seasonings.

Brown Bean Sauce (*tou-pan-chiang* 豆瓣醬)

Fermented lima bean paste mix with malt, flour and salt. Called "*pan* 瓣 , flower petals" because of the shape of lima beans. There are several types, the most popular kind is the spicy one mixed with chili peppers. When the hot type is used, adjust the spiciness according to your taste. There are some kinds with dried shrimp or sesame oil added. Some come with whole beans and in some the beans are mashed. It is a product of Szechuan and used to season those popular regional dishes such as *ma-la-tou-fu* 麻辣豆腐 and *tou-pan-hsien-yü* 豆瓣鮮魚 .

Chili Pepper (*hung-la-chiao* 紅辣椒)

A vegetable used as spice. Should be seeded then minced or shredded before adding to food. After gathering, should be tied up in bunches and hung in an airy place to dry. Pickled chili peppers are called *p'ao-la-chiao* 泡辣椒 , the fermented type with seasoning is *la-chiao-chiang* 辣椒醬 , and with chili pepper oil it is called *la-chiao-yu* 辣椒油 or *la-yu* 辣油 . In "The Masses Cookbook" chili pepper oil was used to stir-fry with vegetables. To make home made *la-chiao-yu*, simply cook 2 minced chili peppers with seeds in 2 table-spoons oil over low heat for 5 minutes until the oil is well flavored, strain the oil and discard peppers.

Brown bean sauce
(*tou-pan-chiang*)

Chili pepper
(*hung-la-chiao*)

Chinese parsley,
fresh coriander
(*hsiang-ts'ai*)

Cinnamon
(*kuei-p'i*)

Chinese Parsley, fresh coriander (*hsiang-ts'ai* 香菜)

Also called *yuan-sui* 芫荽, and the dried seeds are called *yuan-sui-mi* 芫荽米. An herb resembling parsley, belongs to the coriander family. Chopped leaves are used to flavor vegetables and fish soup. Used a great deal in the original book, however, in the English translation trefoil has been substituted for Chinese parsley because of the strong flavor of the latter.

Cinnamon (*kuei-p'i* 桂皮)

Dried aromatic tree bark with mild taste, belongs to the camphor wood family. Broken into small pieces or ground up to add to braised meat dishes. Also a remedy for reducing fever.

Cloves (*ting-hsiang* 丁香)

Dried buds from a type of tropical tree. The Chinese name for cloves is "fragrant nails" because they resemble the Chinese character for "nail." Used either whole or ground in braised pork dishes.

Dried Chinese Black Mushrooms (*tung-ku* 冬菇)

Although *tung-ku* was not used a lot in "The Masses Cookbook," it is an indispensable ingredient in Chinese cooking. The general name for this type of mushrooms is "*tung-ku*" (winter mushrooms). It is so named because they are harvested in the fall and winter. One of the two most frequently used is "*hua-ku* 花菇" which has a thicker cap with cracked lines on the surface. Sometimes referred to as "*hsiang-ku* 香菇" (fragrant mushroom), because it has a fragrant smell. Must soak in water until completely soft before using.

Dried Chinese
black mushrooms
(*tung-ku*)

Fennel seeds
(*hui-hsiang*)

Fennel Seeds (*hui-hsiang* 茴香)

Another Chinese name is *hsiao-hui* 小茴 Good for pork and cookies. Often used as a Chinese herbal medicine, especially for stomach troubles.

Fermented Bean Curd Cake (*fu-ju* 腐乳, *or chiang-tou-fu* 醬豆腐, or *nan-ju* 南乳)

Bean curd fermented in salt, spices, wine and flavoring. There is red fermented bean curd *nan-ju* and white fermented bean curd *fu-ju*. The consistency is soft and creamy. Served as a seasoning to enrich meat or vegetable dishes. Since both types are very salty, should be used with care. Can be served uncooked with congee.

Fermented bean
curd cake
(*fu-i* or *chiang-tou-fu*
or *nan-ju*)

Sold in jars or cans.

Fermented Black Soy Beans (*tou-chi* 豆豉)

Black soy beans fermented with malt, salt and flour. The flavor of the beans is like Japanese *natto*. Mashed or minced then cooked with pork, beef and bean curd to enrich the flavor of the dish.

Five-spice-powder (*wu-hsiang-fên* 五香粉)

A combination of five or six different spices, such as Szechuan peppercorn, clove, cinnamon, fennel, and star anise. Some formulas include Chinese nutmeg (*ts'ao-kuo* 草果) and some have dried orange peel added. When five-spice-powder is mixed with salt it becomes *wu-hsiang-yen* 五香鹽 ; a good condiment for fried food.

Garlic (*suan* 蒜)

Member of lily family. Comes in a bulb like an onion. Each bulb consists of several small sections called cloves. Garlic has a strong and harsh flavor, but when cooked it gives out an aromatic smell. Always added to hot oil before other ingredients in order to permeate the oil. It is said that garlic prolongs life and strengthens health. Should be stored in a dry cool place. Grated raw garlic mixed with soy sauce and other seasonings is an excellent dip for boiled pork and steamed chicken. In "The Masses Cookbook" garlic was used in many dishes. Many recipes in the book used garlic leaves for garnishing. If not available, substitute with scallions or Chinese chives.

Ginger (*chiang* 姜)

A round and knobby root. Has pungent flavor. Should be minced and cooked in hot oil when stir-frying with meat or vegetable, and crushed to release the flavor when adding to stew. Chinese use ginger root also as a medicine to cure indigestion and cold.

Oyster Sauce (*hao-yu* 蠔油)

One of the more expensive Chinese seasonings. It is made by cooking and fermenting the liquid extracted from salted oysters. In "The Masses Cookbook" oyster sauce was not used, however it should be mentioned, because it is an important ingredient in Cantonese cooking. It has a rich and unique flavor. A small amount added to vegetable or bean curd dishes heightens the flavor.

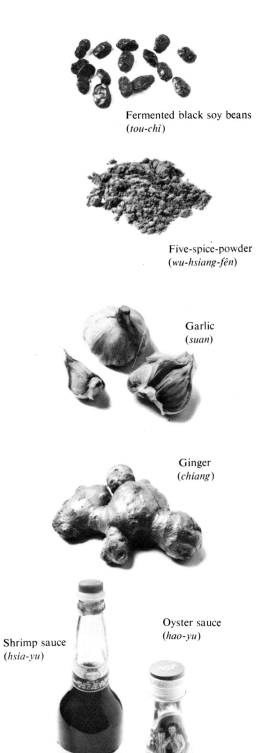

Fermented black soy beans (*tou-chi*)

Five-spice-powder (*wu-hsiang-fên*)

Garlic (*suan*)

Ginger (*chiang*)

Oyster sauce (*hao-yu*)

Shrimp sauce (*hsia-yu*)

13

Pressed Bean Curd (*tou-fu-kan* 豆腐干)

Pressed bean curd is a firmer form of bean curd. One of the major ingredients in Chinese cooking. There are various kinds of *tou-fu-kan* in China. When seasoned with soy sauce and spices it becomes *hsiang-tou-fu-kan*
Can be shredded and served cold mixed in salad or stir-fried with vegetables. When it is not available, fried bean curd may be substituted. Soak fried bean curd in hot water and remove oil before using.

Scallion or Green Onion (*ts'ung* 葱)

A vegetable used for flavoring food. There are many varieties of green onion in China, ranging from very thin to thick. Should be chopped or sliced for stir-frying and cut into sections then crushed for stewing.

Sesame Seed Paste (*chih-ma-chiang* 芝麻醬)

Chinese love the taste of sesame seeds. Sesame oil is often added to their dishes. Sesame seed paste looks like peanut butter. Available in jars. Mixed into sauces for boiled meat, or blended with flour for making Chinese cookies.

Shrimp Sauce (*hsia-yu* 蝦油)

Is the liquid from fermenting shrimp paste (*hsia-chiang* 蝦醬). Shrimp sauce is used as salting agent for vegetable and bean curd dishes. Available in bottles.

Star Anise (*ta-hui* 大茴)

Also called *ta-hui-hsiang* 大茴香 or *pa-chiao* 八角 , and in Peking it is called *ta-liao* 大料
Belongs to the *mu-lan* 木欄 magnolia family, each section of a star anise contains one seed. Has a distinctive taste, used to flavor stewed meat dishes such as *tung-po-jou* 東坡肉 . Also used as a remedy for curing stomach troubles.

Straw-mushrooms (*ts'ao-ku* 草菇)

A kind of mushrooms grown in the spring time. Canned and dried ones are easier to obtain than fresh ones. With a very subtle taste, good with bean curd and soup dishes. Regular fresh of canned mushrooms can be substituted.

Sweet Brown Bean Paste (*tien-mien-chiang* 甜麵醬)

A sweet brown paste made from fermented soy beans, salt and flour. In "The Masses Cookbook" the sauce was used in stir-fried pork and

Preserved bean curd
(*tou-fu-kan*)

Scallion or Green onion
(*ts'ung*)

Sesame seed paste
(*chi-ma-chiang*)

Star anise
(*ta-hui* or *pa-chiao*)

Straw-mushrooms
(*ts'ao-ku*)

vegetable dishes and also added to the sauce for cold noodles and *cha-chiang-mien* noodles.

Szechuan Peppercorns (*hua-chiao* 花椒)

Dried brown peppercorns with a pungent smell. Used both as spice and medicine. Used for redcooked meat dishes. Must be toasted and ground for stir-fried dishes. When mixing ground peppercorns and salt it becomes *hua-chiao-yen* 花椒鹽, used to flavor fried food. To make *hua-chiao-yu* 花椒油, cook 3 tablespoons oil and $1/2$ teaspoon Szechuan peppercorns together for 3 to 4 minutes.

Sweet brown bean paste
(*tien-mien-chiang*)

Szechuan peppercorns
(*hua-chiao*)

Vegetables

Stir-fried Spinach

蝦 油 菠 菜
(Hsia-yu-po-ts'ai)　Shanghai

Ingredients:
1 lb. (500 g) fresh spinach
2 oz. (60 g) canned bamboo shoots
2–3 tablespoons oil
¼ cup chicken stock or water
dash of MSG (optional)
½ teaspoon salt
2 tablespoons shrimp sauce (see page 14)
1 teaspoon sesame oil

Method:
1. Wash spinach and cut crosswise into 1½-inch (5 cm) pieces.
2. Cut bamboo shoots into thin 1-inch (3 cm) by 2-inch (5 cm) slices.

3. Heat oil in a wok or skillet over a high flame, add spinach and bamboo shoots, stir-fry for 1 minute. If liquid in the pan is evaporated, add ¼ cup stock or water. Cover and simmer for 1 minute or until spinach becomes slightly soft.
4. Drain off liquid from pan, add MSG, salt, shrimp sauce and sesame oil to spinach and mix thoroughly. Serve hot.

Note:　In Chinese cooking, stir-fried spinach is often placed around or under some cooked meat. When served with meat, cook spinach without cutting and add more salt or soy sauce according to taste.

Stir-fried Cabbage
素燒卷心菜
(Su-shao-chuan-hsin-ts'ai)　Suchow

Ingredients:
1 lb. (500 g) cabbage
2 teaspoons salt
dash of MSG (optional)
2–3 tablespoons oil
1 cup water

Method:
1. Wash cabbage, remove and discard the tough core. Cut cabbage into 1-inch (3 cm) square pieces.

2. Heat 2–3 tablespoons oil in a wok or skillet over a high flame, drop in cabbage and stir-fry until slightly soft. Add salt, MSG and 1 cup water, cover and simmer for 4–5 minutes. Serve hot.

Note: Cut up fried bean curd (fried *to-fu*), or shredded dried bean curd (*yuba*), or sliced bamboo shoots, or shredded meat, or shredded liver, or dried shrimp may be added. When meat or liver is used, stir-fry it first in a little bit of oil and wine, then add the cabbage.

Cabbage Salad
拌卷心菜
(Pan-chuan-hsin-ts'ai)　Suchow

Ingredients:
½ lb. (250 g) cabbage
Mixture A:
　1½ tablespoons soy sauce
　½ tablespoon sugar
　¼ teaspoon salt
　1 teaspoon sesame oil

Method:
1. In a small bowl combine mixture A.

2. Wash cabbage, remove and discard the tough core. Cut cabbage into 1-inch (2.5 cm) by ½-inch (1.5 cm) pieces.

3. Blanch cabbage in boiling water for 2 minutes and drain thoroughly. Mix cabbage with mixture A and serve.

Note: Soaked and chopped dried shrimp, or shredded *cha-ts'ai* (Szechuan preserved vegetable), or *to-fu-kan* (five-spice pressed bean curd), or chopped chili pepper, or mustard or chili pepper oil may be added to enhance the flavor. When vinegar and more sugar are added to the mixture it will become sweet and sour cabbage.

Braised Chinese Cabbage
熬 白 菜
(Ao-pai-ts'ai)   Peking

Ingredients:

¾ lb. (350 g) Chinese celery cabbage
2 tablespoons dried shrimp (see page 9)
2 tablespoons oil
1 tablespoon chopped scallions
½ teaspoon salt
2½ cups chicken stock

Method:

1. Wash Chinese cabbage thoroughly and drain.
   Cut into 5-inch (16 cm) long by 2-inch (5 cm)
   wide pieces.

2. Rinse dried shrimp and soak in ½ cup of water for 15 minutes.

3. Heat 2 tablespoons oil in a wok or skillet over
   a high flame, drop in scallions, stir and cook
   in hot oil for approximately 10 seconds to
   bring out the flavor. Do not burn scallions.
   Add Chinese cabbage, ½ teaspoon salt, dried
   shrimp along with the soaking water and then
   chicken stock. Cover and simmer for 5 minutes or until cabbage is tender. Serve hot.

Note: This dish can be made into a soup by cutting
the cabbage into small pieces and adding more stock.

Chinese Cabbage with Cream Sauce
抓 奶 汁 白 菜
(Pa-nai-chih-pai-ts'ai)   Tientsin

Ingredients:

½ lb. (250 g) Chinese cabbage
3 tablespoons oil
1 tablespoon chopped scallions
1 teaspoon Chinese rice wine or sake
1 cup chicken stock
pinch of salt
½ cup milk
dash of MSG (optional)
1 tablespoon cornstarch dissolved in 3 tablespoons water
½ teaspoon sesame oil
1–2 slices cooked Smithfield ham, about ⅛-inch
   (3 mm) thick, cut into thin slivers

Method:

1. Wash Chinese cabbage and cut each stalk
   lengthwise into strips about ⅓ inch (1 cm)
   wide.

2. Blanch cabbage in boiling water for 1 minute
   and drain.

3. Heat oil, drop in scallions, stir-fry for 10
   seconds. Add wine, stock, salt and last the
   cabbage, stir well. Bring the stock to a boil
   and cover pan. Turn heat to low and simmer
   for 5 minutes or until tender.

4. Add milk and MSG, mix thoroughly. Bring
   liquid to a boil and thicken sauce with dissolved cornstarch. Transfer cabbage to serving plate and garnish with ham.

Note: Leaf lettuce or iceberg lettuce can be substituted for Chinese cabbage.

19

Chinese Cabbage with Sweet-and-Sour Sauce

醋溜胶菜

(Ts'u-liu-chiao-ts'ai)　Hangchow

Ingredients:

⅔ lb. (300 g) Chinese celery cabbage
1 chili pepper, seeded and chopped
2 tablespoons oil
½ teaspoon Szechuan peppercorns
1 teaspoon cornstarch dissolved in 1 tablespoon
　water
Mixture A:
　½ tablespoon soy sauce
　1 tablespoon vinegar
　½ tablespoon sugar

Method:

1. Remove and discard wilted leaves from cab-
　bage. Separate stalks and wash thoroughly,
　then cut into 1-inch (3 cm) by 2-inch (6 cm)
　pieces.

2. Heat oil, add Szechuan peppercorns, stir in
　hot oil, making sure not to burn them. With
　a slotted spoon remove and discard pepper-
　corns.

3. Reheat the oil in pan over high heat, add
　chili pepper and cabbage, stir and cook for
　2 minutes. Add mixture A and blend well.
　Stir in dissolved cornstarch, cook until sauce
　is thickened.

Note: This dish should be cooked quickly in order
to retain the freshness of the cabbage.

Simmered Chinese Mustard Cabbage

燒青菜

(Shao-ch'ing-ts'ai)　Suchow

Ingredients:

1 lb. (500 g) Chinese mustard cabbage
3 tablespoons oil
1 cup water
2 teaspoons salt
dash of MSG (optional)

Method:

1. Trim off and discard leaves from mustard
　cabbage. Separate stalks and wash thorough-
　ly. Cut stalks crosswise into 2-inch (6 cm)
　sections.

2. Heat oil in a wok, add mustard cabbage and
　stir-fry 1 minute. Add 1 cup water, cover and
　simmer for 2 minutes.

3. Add salt and MSG. Drain off most of the liquid
　and serve.

Note: Cooked ham or dried shrimp may be added.
Substitute fresh asparagus for Chinese mustard cabbage.

Cucumber Salad

糖醋拌黄瓜

(*T'ang-t'su-pan-huang-kua*)　Shanghai

Ingredients:

2 medium cucumbers
1 teaspoon minced fresh ginger
1 teaspoon sesame oil
Mixture A:
　2 tablespoons vinegar
　1½ tablespoons sugar

Method:

1. Peel cucumbers and cut in two lengthwise. Scrape out seeds. Cut into pieces 1 inch (3 cm) long by ½ inch (1.5 cm) wide.

2. Mix cucumbers with ginger and sesame oil, place on a plate and pour mixture A over just before serving.

Note: One teaspoon of soy sauce, or 1 teaspoon toasted Szechuan peppercorns, or Szechuan peppercorn powder, or chopped chili pepper may be added to mixture A.

Stir-fried Cucumber with Shrimp

黄瓜炒子蝦

(*Huang-kua-ch'ao-tzǔ-hsia*)　Shanghai

Ingredients:

2 medium cucumbers
⅓ lb. (150 g) small shrimp
3 tablespoons oil
½ tablespoon Chinese rice wine or sake
Mixture A:
　1½ tablespoons soy sauce
　1 tablespoon sugar
　¼ teaspoon salt

Method:

1. Wash cucumbers, (peel, if skin is tough), cut lengthwise in two, remove seeds. Cut each half crosswise into slices ¼ inch (6 mm) thick.

2. Shell and devein shrimp. Wash thoroughly and drain.

3. Heat oil, add shrimp and stir-fry over high heat for 1 minute, add wine and mix well. When shrimp become slightly firm, add cucumbers and mixture A. Cook and stir for 2 minutes.

Note: In the original version, river shrimp with roe is used, but any small shrimp can be used in this recipe.

Carrot Salad

拌 胡 羅 蔔 絲
(Pan-hú-lo-po-ssŭ)   Chengtu

Ingredients:
1 lb. (500 g) carrots
2 teaspoons salt
3 tablespoons chopped fresh coriander
3 tablespoons chopped chives or leeks
Mixture A:
  1 tablespoon vinegar
  4 tablespoons vegetable oil
  1 teaspoon *la-chiao-chiang* (chili pepper paste, page 11)
  2 teaspoons sesame oil
  1½ tablespoons sugar
  1 teaspoon salt

Method:
1. Shred carrots, or cut into slivers about 2 inches (5 cm) long. Place in a colander and mix in 2 teaspoons salt and let stand for 20 minutes.

2. In a small bowl combine mixture A.

3. Rinse carrots and drain. Add mixture A, fresh coriander and chives, blend thoroughly and serve.

Note: Chili pepper oil may be substituted for chili pepper paste.

Celery Salad

22

Stir-fried Celery
with Pork
炒芹菜
(Ch'ao-ch'in-ts'ai) Peking

Ingredients:

1 lb. (500 g) celery
⅓ lb. (150 g) pork
Mixture A:
   1 tablespoon light soy sauce
   1 teaspoon sugar
   1 teaspoon cornstarch
4 tablespoons oil
½ teaspoon Szechuan peppercorns
1 tablespoon minced scallions
1 tablespoon light soy sauce
½ teaspoon salt

Method:

1. Separate celery stalks, remove and discard leaves and stringy parts. Cut each stalk into pieces ½ inch (1.5 cm) wide by 2 inches (6 cm) long.

2. Slice pork into thin pieces ½ inch (1.5 cm) wide by 2 inches (6 cm) long and mix thoroughly with mixture A.

3. Heat 2 tablespoons oil and stir-fry pork for about 2 minutes. Transfer to plate.

4. Heat the remaining 2 tablespoons of oil in a pan, add Szechuan peppercorns and cook until brown, remove and discard peppercorns with a slotted spoon. Add scallions and celery to peppercorn oil and stir-fry for a couple of minutes. Add pork, soy sauce and salt, then blend everything thoroughly and serve.

Note: This dish can be served as a main dish. When pork is omitted, plain stir-fried celery can accompany meat dishes.

Celery Salad
拌芹菜
(Pan-ch'in-ts'ai) Suchow

Ingredients:

1 lb. (500 g) celery
¼ teaspoon salt
Mixture A:
   1½ tablespoons light soy sauce
   1 tablespoon sesame oil
   1 teaspoon salt
   1 teaspoon sugar

Method:

1. Separate stalks of celery, remove and discard the leaves. Rinse thoroughly and drain. Cut each stalk diagonally into thin 2-inch (5 cm) pieces.

2. In a small bowl combine mixture A.

3. In a large pan bring 8 cups of water to a boil and blanch celery for 15 seconds, remove from water and drain.

4. Mix celery with mixture A and let stand for 30 minutes before serving.

Eggplant Salad
拌茄泥
(Pan-ch'ieh-ni)   Peking

Ingredients:
¾ lb. (350 g) eggplants
1 teaspoon minced garlic
1 teaspoon chives or scallions, chopped
1 teaspoon minced fresh coriander
Mixture A:
  2 tablespoons *chi-ma-chiang* (sesame paste,
    page 14)
  ½ teaspoon salt
  1 teaspoon sesame oil
  1 tablespoon soy sauce
  1 tablespoon vinegar
  1 teaspoon sugar

Method:
1. Wash eggplants and remove stems. If the diameter of eggplants is over 2 inches (6 cm), cut each eggplant lengthwise in two. Steam for 15 minutes or until a toothpick can go through easily. Remove from pan and cool.

2. In a small bowl combine mixture A, and stir in garlic, chives and coriander.

3. Tear eggplants lengthwise with hand into narrow strips and arrange neatly on a plate. Pour mixture A and the herbs over them and serve.

Fried Eggplants in Brown Bean Sauce
醬爆茄子
(Chiang-pao-ch'ieh-tzŭ)   Shanghai

Ingredients:
1 lb. (500 g) eggplants
4 cups oil for deep-frying
1 teaspoon minced fresh ginger
Mixture A:
  2 tablespoons soy sauce
  2½ tablespoons *t'ien-mien-chiang* (sweet
    brown bean paste, page 14)
  ⅓ teaspoon sugar
  dash of MSG (optional)
  1 teaspoon cornstarch dissolved in 1 tablespoon water

Method:
1. Wash eggplants. Cut off stems from both ends, then without peeling, cut into slices about 1 inch (3 cm) thick. Cut the slices into 1 inch (3 cm) square strips about 4 inches (12 cm) long.

2. In a wok heat oil until very hot, deep-fry eggplants for 30 seconds, remove from oil and drain.

3. Empty all but 3 tablespoons of oil from wok, heat till hot. Stir in ginger, add eggplants and mixture A. Cook and stir over low heat for 30 seconds, thicken with dissolved cornstarch.

Note: One teaspoon minced garlic and 1 tablespoon chopped scallions may be added with the ginger.

24

5. Heat the remaining 3 tablespoons of oil and add garlic, cook in hot oil for about 30 seconds. Add mixture A and bring to a boil. Place stuffed eggplants in the sauce and cook covered over medium heat for 10 minutes. Thicken sauce with dissolved cornstarch and serve.

Eggplants Stuffed with Meat and Fish

煎 鑲 鮮 茄 子

(Chien-hsiang-hsien-ch'ieh-tzŭ)　Canton

Ingredients:

1 lb. (500 g) eggplants, about 2 inches (5 cm) in diameter

¼ lb. (175 g) fish fillet

¼ lb. (175 g) ground pork

1 tablespoon cornstarch

½ teaspoon salt

6 tablespoons oil

1 tablespoon minced garlic

1 teaspoon cornstarch dissolved in 1 tablespoon water

Mixture A:

  1½ tablespoons light soy sauce

  1 teaspoon salt

  1 teaspoon ground soy bean paste

  1 tablespoon sugar

  ¾ cup water

Method:

1. Wash eggplants. Without peeling, slice into pieces ½ inch (1.5 cm) thick. Soak in cold water for 10 minutes and drain.

2. Chop fish fillet until very fine. In a large bowl combine fish, ground pork, 1 tablespoon cornstarch and ½ teaspoon salt. Stir and beat until mixture becomes elastic.

3. Dust one side of each slice of eggplant with cornstarch. Spread a ½-inch (1 cm) layer of meat mixture on the dusted side, then stick another slice of eggplant with the dusted side down onto the meat, making an eggplant sandwich.

4. Heat 3 tablespoons oil in a skillet and brown both sides of stuffed eggplants. Remove from oil and set aside.

Eggplants with Chili Pepper Sauce

辣 味 茄 絲

(La-wei-ch'ieh-ssŭ)　Shanghai

Ingredients:

⅔ lb. (300 g) eggplants

3 tablespoons oil

1 teaspoon minced fresh ginger

Mixture A:

  1½ tablespoons soy sauce

  1 teaspoon *la-chiao-chiang* (chili pepper paste, page 11)

  1 teaspoon sugar

  dash of MSG (optional)

  ½ cup chicken stock

Method:

1. Cut eggplants into thin strips about 2 inches (5 cm) long.

2. Heat oil, add ginger and eggplants. With a spatula toss eggplants thoroughly in hot oil, add mixture A. Reduce heat and cook for 3 minutes. If there is still quite a lot of liquid in the pan, turn the fire up to high and cook rapidly until most of the liquid is evaporated. Add 1 more tablespoon oil to eggplants and serve.

Stir-fried Tomatoes

炒西紅柿
(Ch'ao-hsi-hung-shih)　Peking

Ingredients:
1 lb. (500 g) tomatoes
3 tablespoons oil
2 tablespoons chopped scallions
Mixture A:
　1 teaspoon soy sauce
　1 tablespoon sugar
　½ teaspoon salt

Method:
1. Soak tomatoes in boiling water for 30 seconds and peel off skins. Cut tomatoes lengthwise from top to bottom in two, remove stems and seeds. Cut each half lengthwise into ½-inch (1.5 cm) wedges.

2. Heat oil, add scallions and cook for 30 seconds, add tomatoes and mixture A. With a spatula stir and turn tomatoes constantly for 1 minute. Remove from heat and serve.

Note: Overripe tomatoes or prolonged cooking should be avoided for they will make the dish too mushy. This dish should be cooked very quickly over high heat.

Tomatoes with Meat Sauce

肉 松 蕃 茄

(Jou-sung-fang-ch'ieh)   Shanghai

Ingredients:
1 lb. (500 g) tomatoes
2 oz. (60 g) ground pork
cornstarch for dusting
3 tablespoons oil
Mixture A:
  1 tablespoon tomato ketchup
  1 teaspoon sugar
  1 teaspoon *la-chiao-chiang* (chili pepper paste, page 11)
  1 teaspoon salt

Method:
1. Stir-fry ground pork with 1 tablespoon oil and set aside.

2. Soak tomatoes in boiling water for 30 seconds and peel off skins. Cut tomatoes crosswise into ½-inch (1.5 cm) slices. Dredge lightly in cornstarch.

3. Heat 2 tablespoons oil in a skillet, fry tomatoes one layer at a time for 15 seconds on each side. Add pork, mixture A and 3 tablespoons water, simmer for 10 seconds. Transfer tomatoes to plate and pour the meat sauce over them.

Tomatoes with Cream Sauce

奶 油 蕃 茄

(Nai-yu-fan-ch'ieh)   Hangchow

Ingredients:
1 lb. (500 g) tomatoes
⅓ oz. (10 g) chicken fat *(chi-yu)*
Mixture A:
  1 cup milk
  1 teaspoon cornstarch
  dash of MSG (optional)

Method:
1. Soak tomatoes in boiling water for 30 seconds and peel off skins. Cut tomatoes lengthwise from top to bottom into 6 wedges. Remove stems and seeds.

2. In a wok bring 1½ cups water to a boil over high heat. Add tomatoes and bring to a boil again, add mixture A, stir and cook until sauce becomes slightly thick. Blend in chicken fat, then transfer to a plate and serve.

Stir-fried Green Peppers
生煸青椒
(Shêng-pien-ch'ing-chiao)　Suchow

Ingredients:
6 small green peppers
3 tablespoons oil
½ teaspoon salt
½ teaspoon sugar

Method:
1. Cut green peppers in two, remove stems and seeds, then cut peppers into ½-inch (1.5 cm) squares.
2. Heat oil, add green peppers and stir-fry for 30 seconds. Add salt, sugar and 2 tablespoons water, cook and stir constantly for another 2 minutes.

Note: When very tender green peppers are used, shorten cooking time. A few seconds of stirring and cooking after seasoning has been added should be sufficient.

Stir-fried Green Peppers with Fermented Black Beans
青椒炒豆豉
(Ch'ing-chiao-ch'ao-tou-ch'ih)　Chengtu

Ingredients:
8 small green peppers
2 tablespoons *tou-ch'ih* (fermented black beans)
3 tablespoons oil
1 tablespoon soy sauce
1 teaspoon sugar

Method:
1. Cut green peppers lengthwise in two, remove stems and seeds, then cut into thin strips.
2. Rinse and mince fermented black beans.
3. Heat 2 tablespoons oil, stir-fry green peppers until soft. Transfer to a plate.
4. Heat the remaining oil, add fermented black beans and stir in hot oil for 30 seconds. Add green peppers, soy sauce and sugar.

Note: Fermented black beans give a distinctive flavor to this quick and easy dish.

Braised Giant White Radish

干燒菜頭

(Kan-shao-ts'ai-t'ou)　Hangchow

Ingredients:
1 lb. (500 g) giant white radish
2 teaspoons dried shrimp
3 tablespoons oil
1 teaspoon minced fresh ginger
1 chili pepper, seeded and minced
2 oz. (50 g) ground pork
1 teaspoon chopped scallions
Mixture A:
　1 tablespoon Chinese rice wine
　　or sake
　3 tablespoons soy sauce
　dash of MSG (optional)

Method:
1. Soak dried shrimp in lukewarm water for 30 minutes and mince.

2. Peel and cut radish lengthwise into large strips 1-inch (3 cm) square, then cut each strip diagonally into 2-inch (6 cm) sections.

3. Heat oil, stir in ginger and chili pepper, cook in hot oil for 30 seconds. Add dried shrimp, ground pork, radish, mixture A and 1 cup of water. Stir and blend everything thoroughly. Cover and simmer over a low flame until radish is tender. Transfer to a serving plate and garnish with chopped scallions.

Note: One teaspoon of sugar may be added to mixture A.

Giant White Radish and Shrimp Soup

開洋羅蔔絲湯

(K'ai-yang-lo-po-ssŭ-t'ang)　Hangchow

Ingredients:
¼ lb. (100 g) giant white radish
2 tablespoons dried shrimp
2 tablespoons oil
1 tablespoon chopped scallions
1 tablespoon Chinese rice wine
　or sake
4 cups chicken stock or water
1 teaspoon salt
dash of MSG (optional)

Method:
1. Soak dried shrimp in cold water for 20 minutes.

2. Peel and shred radish.

3. Heat 1 tablespoon oil, add scallions and cook for 30 seconds. Pour in wine and stock or water, then add radish and dried shrimp. Cover pan and cook for 10 minutes or until radish is tender. Add salt and MSG. Just before serving add 1 tablespoon oil to soup.

Sweet-and-Sour Lotus Roots

糖醋炒藕絲
(T'ang-ts'u-ch'ao-ou-ssŭ)   Hangchow

Ingredients:

1 lb. (500 g) fresh lotus root
2 tablespoons oil
½ teaspoon Szechuan peppercorns (see page 15)
1 teaspoon cornstarch dissolved in 1 tablespoon water
Mixture A:
   2 tablespoons vinegar
   1 tablespoon light soy sauce
   2 tablespoons sugar
   ½ teaspoon salt

Method:

1. Wash and peel lotus root. Cut crosswise into 2-inch (6 cm) sections, then cut each section lengthwise into thin slivers. In a large bowl mix 5 cups of water with 2 tablespoons vinegar and soak sliced lotus root for 15 minutes and drain.

2. Heat oil, add Szechuan peppercorns and cook until peppercorns become dark brown. With a slotted spoon, remove and discard peppercorns. Add lotus roots and mixture A to the peppercorn oil and stir-fry for 1 minute. Stir in dissolved cornstarch and cook until sauce becomes thick.

Note: Thinly sliced pork may be added to this recipe as shown in the picture.

Stir-fried Bamboo Shoots
干燒筍
(Kan-shao-sun) Suchow

Ingredients:

⅔ lb. (300 g) canned bamboo shoots
1 tablespoon dried shrimp
1 oz. (30 g) *cha-ts'ai* (Szechuan preserved vegetable, page 8)
1 chili pepper, chopped
oil for deep-frying
2 oz. (50 g) ground pork
1 teaspoon sesame oil
1 tablespoon chopped scallions
Mixture A:
  2 tablespoons soy sauce
  1 teaspoon sugar
  2–3 tablespoons water

Method:

1. Cut bamboo shoots into pieces 1½ inches (4.5 cm) long by ½ inch (1.5 cm) thick.

2. In a small bowl cover dried shrimp with water and soak for 30 minutes. Rinse Szechuan preserved vegetable and chop.

3. Heat oil, deep-fry bamboo shoots for about 1 minute, remove from oil and drain.

4. Empty all but 2 tablespoons of oil from pan, add ground pork, cook and separate pork in oil. Add dried shrimp, Szechuan preserved vegetable and chili pepper. Mix all the ingredients thoroughly, then add bamboo shoots, chopped scallions and mixture A. Stir and cook for 30 seconds, mix in sesame oil and serve.

Fried Bamboo Shoots with Pickled Mustard Greens
炒雪筍
(Ch'ao-hsüeh-sun) Suchow

Ingredients:

⅔ lb. (300 g) canned bamboo shoots
¼ lb. (100 g) *hsüeh-ts'ai* (red-in-snow or pickled mustard greens, page 9)
oil for deep-frying
1 teaspoon cornstarch dissolved in 1 tablespoon water
1 teaspoon sesame oil
Mixture A:
  ½ cup chicken stock
  1 teaspoon sugar
  ½ teaspoon salt

Method:

1. Cut bamboo shoots into small wedges.

2. Soak pickled mustard greens in water for 15 minutes. Rinse and squeeze to remove excess water, then chop into fine pieces.

3. Heat 3–4 cups of oil until very hot and deep-fry bamboo shoots for about 1 minute, remove from oil and drain.

4. Empty all the oil from pan, with the same pan bring mixture A to a boil. Add bamboo shoots and simmer for 10 minutes over a slow fire. Turn the heat up to high, add pickled mustard greens and thicken sauce with dissolved cornstarch. Mix in sesame oil and serve.

Potato Pancakes Chinese Style

什錦薯餅
(Shih-chin-shu-ping)   Shanghai

Ingredients:

⅔ lb. (300 g) potatoes
5 tablespoons oil
1 tablespoon chopped scallions
2 oz. (50 g) ground pork
1 teaspoon soy sauce
2 teaspoons white seasame seeds
4–5 tablespoons cornstarch
Mixture A:
  ½ teaspoon salt
  dash of white pepper
  1 teaspoon sesame oil
  1 tablespoon cornstarch

Method:

1. Boil potatoes until soft. Peel and mash potatoes while they are still hot.

2. Heat 1 tablespoon oil and stir-fry scallions for 30 seconds, add pork and stir to separate the meat. Add soy sauce, mix well then transfer to a plate.

3. In an ungreased cast-iron pan, toast sesame seeds over a low fire for 2 to 3 minutes.

4. Mix mashed potatoes with mixture A, sesame seeds and pork. Divide into 8 portions and make 8 potato pancakes about ⅓ inch (1 cm) thick. Dredge with cornstarch.

5. Heat 4 tablespoons oil and fry potato pancakes until both sides are golden brown.

Note: In the original recipe, the potato pancakes are deep-fried. When for deep-frying, coat pancakes with more cornstarch or with bread crumbs. Also in the original recipe, raw scallions, instead of cooked ones, are mixed in with potatoes to give better flavor to the dish.

Curry Potatoes

咖 喱 洋 山 芋

(Ka-li-yang-shan-yü)   Shanghai

Ingredients:
¾ lb. (350 g) potatoes
3 tablespoons oil
1½ tablespoons curry powder
1 cup chicken stock or water
1 teaspoon salt
dash of MSG (optional)

Method:

1. Wash and peel potatoes. Cut into wedges about 1 inch (3 cm) wide.

2. Heat oil, stir in curry powder, add potatoes, blend to coat potatoes with curry powder. Pour in chicken stock, bring to a boil then cover with lid and simmer for 10 minutes. Add salt and MSG, boil rapidly over high heat until most of the liquid is evaporated.

Note: The length of cooking time depends on the potatoes. Be sure to cook potatoes thoroughly.

Stir-fried Potatoes

炒 土 豆 絲

(Ch'ao-t'u-tou-ssŭ)   Peking

Ingredients:
1 lb. (500 g) potatoes
3 tablespoons oil
½ teaspoon Szechuan peppercorns (see page 15)
1 tablespoon chopped scallions
Mixture A:
   1 tablespoon soy sauce
   1 tablespoon vinegar
   1 teaspoon salt

Method:

1. Wash and peel potatoes. Cut into thin strips and soak in cold water for 15 minutes, drain.

2. In a large saucepan bring 6–8 cups water to a boil, drop in potatoes and boil for 2 minutes. Drain.

3. Heat oil in a wok, add Szechuan peppercorns and cook until peppercorns become dark brown. With a slotted spoon remove and discard peppercorns. Add potatoes and scallions to oil, stir-fry for 2 minutes, add mixture A and blend thoroughly.

Stir-fried Soy Bean Sprouts

素炒黃豆芽
(*Su-ch'ao-huang-tou-ya*)　Suchow

Ingredients:

1 lb. (500 g) soy bean sprouts
3 tablespoons oil
1 tablespoon soy sauce
1 teaspoon sugar

Method:

1. Wash bean sprouts and drain.

2. Heat oil in a wok, add bean sprouts, stir-fry for 1 minute. Add soy sauce, salt and ½ cup water, cover pan and cook for 3 minutes over high heat.

3. Add sugar, toss and cook until liquid is evaporated.

Note:　Soy bean sprouts are larger and tougher than regular mung bean sprouts.
Chopped salted green vegetables or slivered fried bean curd may be added in step 2.

Stir-fried Snow Peas

烟扁豆

(*Men-pien-tou*)　Peking

Ingredients:
¾ lb. (350 g) snow peas
4 tablespoons oil
1 teaspoon salt
1 tablespoon chopped scallions
1 teaspoon minced garlic
1 tablespoon brown bean paste
1 tablespoon soy sauce
1 teaspoon sugar
dash of MSG (optional)
1 teaspoon sesame oil

Method:
1. Snap off both tips of snow peas and remove strings from the sides. Rinse and drain.

2. Heat 2 tablespoons oil, stir-fry snow peas over high heat for 1 minute. Add salt and 1 cup water, then cook covered, for 2 minutes. Drain off liquid and transfer snow peas to plate.

3. Heat the remaining oil, stir in scallions and garlic and cook for 30 seconds. Add snow peas, bean paste, soy sauce, sugar, MSG and sesame oil, mix well and serve.

Note: String beans may be substituted for snow peas.

Stir-fried String Beans

醬烤四季豆

(*Chiang-kao-szu-chi-tou*)　Suchow

Ingredients:
½ lb. (250 g) string beans
2 tablespoons oil
1 tablespoon brown bean paste (*tou-pan-chiang,* page 11)
2 teaspoons soy sauce
1 teaspoon sugar

Method:
1. Wash string beans, snap off and discard the ends, then cut into 2-inch (6 cm) pieces.

2. Heat oil, stir-fry beans for 2 minutes. Add ⅔ cup water, cover and cook for 3 minutes.

3. Add brown bean sauce and soy sauce, cook and stir until beans are tender but still crisp. Sprinkle with sugar and cook over high heat until liquid is evaporated.

Note: Chili peppers or chili pepper oil can be added in step 3 for those who like spicy food.

Braised Green Peas

白 油 烩 碗 豆
(Pai-yu-hui-wan-tou)　Chengtu

Ingredients:
1 lb. (500 g) fresh green peas in their shells, or 1
　package defrosted frozen peas
2 tablespoons oil
2 cups chicken stock
1 tablespoon Chinese rice wine or sake
¼ teaspoon salt
½ teaspoon sugar
½ tablespoon cornstarch dissolved in 2 table-
　spoons water

Method:
1. Shell green peas. Rinse and drain.
2. Heat 2 tablespoons oil, stir-fry green peas
　 over moderate heat for 1 minute. Add stock
　 and wine, cover and simmer for 5 minutes.
3. Uncover pan, stir in salt and sugar. Then
　 thicken sauce with dissolved cornstarch.

Note:　The name *pai-yu* here means "seasoned with
salt," but this dish may be seasoned with soy sauce.
When ground pork is added in step 2, this dish can
be served as a main dish.

Stir-fried Lima Beans

青煸鮮蚕豆

(Ch'ing-pien-hsien-ts'an-tou)   Suchow

Ingredients:

1½ lb. (750 g) fresh lima beans in their shells, or 1 package defrosted frozen lima beans
2 tablespoons oil
2 tablespoons sugar
1 teaspoon salt
2 tablespoons chopped scallions

Method:

1. Shell lima beans. Rinse and drain.

2. Heat oil, stir-fry lima beans for 3 minutes or until the skins start to come apart. Add sugar and salt, and cook for 2–3 minutes more. Mix in scallions and stir everything a few more times. Serve hot or cold.

Note: For sweet-and-sour lima beans, parboil lima beans, then stir-fry in 2 tablespoons oil for 3 minutes. In a bowl combine 1 teaspoon minced garlic, 1 teaspoon minced fresh ginger, ½ teaspoon Szechuan peppercorn powder, 2 tablespoons vinegar, 1 tablespoon sugar, pinch of salt and 3 tablespoons hot water, mix thoroughly. Mix cooked lima beans with the sweet-and-sour sauce and garnish with 1 tablespoon chopped scallions and serve.

Stir-fried Fresh Soy Beans

青椒香干炒毛豆

(Ch'ing-chiao-hsiang-kan-ch'ao-mao-tou)
Suchow

Ingredients:

¼ lb. (100 g) green peppers
¼ lb. (100 g) fresh soy beans
1 piece fried bean curd about 3″×5″ (7.5×12 cm)
2 tablespoons oil
1 teaspoon sesame oil
Mixture A:
  ½ teaspoon salt
  1 teaspoon sugar
  dash of MSG

Method:

1. Cut green peppers in two lengthwise, remove and discard stems and seeds, then cut peppers into thin slivers.

2. Cut fried bean curd into thin strips.

3. Heat oil, stir-fry green peppers and fresh soy beans for 2 minutes. Add fried bean curd and mixture A. Stir and cook until liquid is evaporated, add sesame oil and serve.

Note: In the original recipe, five-spice-pressed bean curd is used instead of fried bean curd.

Stir-fried Matrimony Vine

生煸枸杞
(Shêng-pien-kou-ch'i)　Suchow

Ingredients:

1 lb. (500 g) *kou-ch'i* (matrimony vine)
3 tablespoons oil
Mixture A:
  1 teaspoon salt
  1 teaspoon soy sauce
  2 tablespoons sugar
  2 tablespoons chicken stock or water

Method:

1. Strip leaves from matrimony vine, discard stems and reserve the leaves.

2. Heat oil and stir-fry the leaves over high heat for 1 minute, blend in mixture A and serve.

Note: Shredded bamboo shoots or sliced mushrooms may be added to the leaves.
Matrimony vine belongs to the eggplant family. It sprouts in the spring and bears red fruit in the fall. It is believed to be good for diabetes and for kidney and stomach troubles. It is also said to help prolong life.

    Both the fruit and the leaves are used for making either soup or wine.

Winter Melon Soup with Hsueh-ts'ai

雪菜冬瓜湯

(Hsüeh-ts'ai-tung-kua-t'ang) Shanghai

Ingredients:

1 lb. (500 g) winter melon
2 oz. (50 g) *hsüeh-ts'ai* (red-in-snow or pickled mustard greens, page 9)
4–5 cups chicken stock
¼ teaspoon salt
dash of MSG (optional)
1 teaspoon oil

Method:

1. Peel winter melon and remove seeds. Slice melon into 1½-inch (4 cm) squares and about 1 inch (3 cm) thick.

2. Boil winter melon in water for 3 minutes, rinse with cold water and drain.

3. Wash red-in-snow or pickled mustard greens and chop.

4. In a large pan bring to a boil 4–5 cups of stock, winter melon and pickled mustard greens. Add salt and MSG, then cover pan and simmer for 2 minutes, add oil before serving.

Winter Melon Soup with Shrimp

開洋冬瓜湯

(K'ai-yang-tung-kua-t'ang) Shanghai

Ingredients:

1 lb. (500 g) winter melon
1 tablespoon dried shrimp
4–5 cups chicken stock
1 teaspoon salt
1 teaspoon chopped scallions
dash of MSG (optional)
½ teaspoon oil

Method:

1. Peel winter melon and remove seeds. Slice melon into pieces 1 inch (3 cm) by 2 inches (6 cm) and about ¼ inch (6 mm) thick.

2. In a small bowl cover dried shrimp with water and soak for 30 minutes.

3. In a kettle bring to a boil chicken stock, winter melon, dried shrimp and salt. Then lower heat and simmer for 20 minutes. Add chopped scallions, MSG and oil.

Note: Winter melon is said to be good for hypertension. This pumpkin-sized melon does not have much flavor of its own. Available in the summer and in the fall. Winter melon can be stir-fried with soy sauce or cooked and served with a cream sauce.

Bean Curd

Bean Curd with Ground Meat

麻 辣 豆 腐
(*Ma-la-tou-fu*)　Chungking

Ingredients:

2 squares bean curd 3″ × 3″ (7.5 × 7.5 cm)
1 tablespoon mashed fermented black beans
　(*tou-ch'ih*, page 13)
1 chili pepper, seeded and chopped
2 tablespoons oil
1 tablespoon minced scallions
1 teaspoon minced garlic
¼ lb. (25 g) ground beef
2 teaspoons cornstarch dissolved in 2 table-
　spoons water
pinch of Szechuan peppercorn powder (optional)
Mixture A:
　1 tablespoon soy sauce
　1 tablespoon ground brown beans
　½ cup chicken stock

Method:

1. Cut bean curd into pieces ½-inch (1.5 cm)
   square.

2. Heat oil, add scallions, garlic and chili pepper,
   cook for 30 seconds. Add mashed fermented
   black beans and beef, stir-fry until the beef
   is no longer pink. Add bean curd and gently
   stir in mixture A, cover pan and cook over
   low heat for 15 minutes. Agitate the pan occasionally for even cooking.

3. Thicken sauce with dissolved cornstarch,
   transfer bean curd to plate and sprinkle with
   Szechuan peppercorn powder.

Note: Cayenne powder can be used instead of fresh
chili pepper. For those who prefer a milder taste use
less chili pepper. One teaspoon sugar added to mixture A will enhance the flavor of the dish.

Bean Curd with Mo-ku
蘑 菇 燉 豆 腐
(Mo-ku-t'un-tou-fu)   Hangchow

Ingredients:
2 squares bean curd, about 3″ × 3″ (7.5 × 7.5 cm) each
½ lb. (250 g) canned bamboo shoots
1 cup chicken stock
½ teaspoon salt
1 tablespoon Chinese rice wine or sake
2 oz. (50 g) canned *mo-ku* or champignons (see page 12)
a few drops of sesame oil
dash of MSG (optional)
2 teaspoons cornstarch dissolved in 2 tablespoons water
1 tablespoon chopped scallions

Method:
1. Cut bean curd into ⅔-inch (2 cm) cubes, and let stand on a chopping board to drain.
2. Slice bamboo shoots into thin ⅔-inch (2 cm) squares.
3. In a pot bring to a boil bean curd, stock, salt, wine, bamboo shoots and *mo-ku*. Cover, and simmer for 20 minutes.
4. Add sesame oil and MSG, then thicken sauce with dissolved cornstarch. Transfer to serving plate and garnish with chopped scallions.

Bean Curd Soup with Mushrooms and Bamboo Shoots
滷 煮 豆 腐
(Lu-chu-tou-fu)   Tsingtao

Ingredients:
1 square bean curd about 3″ × 3″ (7.5 × 7.5 cm)
4 dried Chinese mushrooms (*tung-ku*, page 12)
¼ cup sliced canned bamboo shoots
3 slices cooked Smithfield ham, about ⅛ inch (3 mm) thick
2 tablespoons oil
1 tablespoon chopped scallions
2½ cups chicken stock
2 tablespoons soy sauce
1 teaspoon Chinese rice wine or sake
2 tablespoons soy sauce
1 teaspoon Chinese rice wine or sake
dash of MSG (optional)
a few drops of sesame oil

Method:
1. Cut bean curd into 1½-inch (4 cm) cubes and about ⅓ inch (1 cm) thick. Then cut each cube diagonally into 2 triangles.
2. Soak mushrooms in lukewarm water for 20 minutes, remove and discard stems. Cut large ones in two.
3. Slice ham into 1-inch (3 cm) squares.
4. Heat oil, stir in scallions and cook for 30 seconds. Add bean curd, mushrooms, bamboo shoots, ham, chicken stock, soy sauce and wine. Bring everything to a boil, skim off scum if any. Add sesame oil and MSG, serve hot.

Bean Curd
with Tomatoes

蕃茄燒豆腐
(*Fan-ch'ieh-shao-tou-fu*)　Chengtu

Ingredients:

2 squares bean curd, about 3″ × 3″ (7.5 × 7.5 cm) each
2 tomatoes
2 tablespoons oil
1½ cups chicken stock
1 tablespoon Chinese rice wine or sake
1½ tablespoons sugar
1 teaspoon salt
dash of pepper
dash of MSG (optional)
2 teaspoons cornstarch dissolved in 2 tablespoons water
½ tablespoon chicken oil (optional)
1 tablespoon chopped scallions

Method:

1. Cut bean curd into 1-inch (3 cm) by ½-inch (1.5 cm) pieces, about ½-inch (1.5 cm) thick. Peel tomatoes and remove stems and seeds, cut into ½-inch (1.5 cm) cubes.

2. Heat oil, add tomatoes and stir-fry over high heat. Add bean curd, stock, wine, sugar, salt, pepper and MSG. Stir-fry gently and blend all the ingredients thoroughly. Thicken sauce with dissolved cornstarch, add chicken oil. Transfer the whole thing to a plate and garnish with chopped scallions.

Note: Chicken oil is made by rendering fresh chicken fat over a low fire.

Stir-fried Bean Curd with Preserved Cucumbers

炒豆腐松
(*Ch'ao-tou-fu-sung*)　Shanghai　very good

Ingredients:

2 squares bean curd, about 3″ × 3″ (7.5 × 7.5 cm) each
2 tablespoons oil
2 tablespoons minced preserved cucumbers
2 tablespoons minced pickled ginger
¼ teaspoon salt
1½ tablespoons soy sauce
1½ tablespoons sugar
dash of MSG (optional)
2 teaspoons chopped scallions

Method:

1. Rinse bean curd, wrap with cheesecloth, then squeeze by hands to break apart the bean curd, drain off excess liquid.

2. Heat oil, stir-fry bean curd for 2 minutes. With a spatula, cut bean curd into smaller pieces, turn and stir constantly. Cook bean curd until liquid is completely evaporated and bean curd becomes slightly brown. Add preserved cucumbers, pickled ginger, sugar, MSG and scallions. Blend well and serve.

Bean Curd with Cucumbers

very good

絲 瓜 豆 腐

(Ssŭ-kua-tou-fu)   Shanghai

Ingredients:

2 small cucumbers (or zucchini)
2 squares bean curd, about 3″ × 3″ (7.5 × 7.5 cm) each
3 tablespoons oil
1½ tablespoons soy sauce
1 tablespoon sugar
½ tablespoon chopped scallions
½ cup chicken stock
dash of MSG (optional)
2 teaspoons cornstarch dissolved in 1 table-spoon water
½ tablespoon lard (optional)
1 C. Szechuan chili bean paste.

Method:

1. Peel cucumbers, quarter lengthwise, then cut diagonally into 1-inch (2.5 cm) sections.

2. Dice bean curd.

3. Heat oil, stir-fry cucumbers for 2 minutes. Add soy sauce, sugar, scallions, stock and bean curd, bring to a boil. Cover pan and simmer for 2 minutes or until bean curd floats to the top. Turn heat to high and cook for 30 seconds more, add MSG, then thicken sauce with dissolved cornstarch.

Note: In this recipe cucumbers are substituted for the Chinese okra (pleated squash).

Bean Curd with Salted Cabbage

鹽 擠 燒 豆 腐

(Yen-chi-shao-tou-fu)   Suchow

Ingeredients:

5 oz. (150 g) salted cabbage or red-in-snow (pickled mustard greens, page 9)
2 squares bean curd, about 3″ × 3″ (7.5 × 7.5 cm) each
3 tablespoons oil
2 tablespoons soy sauce
1 teaspoon sugar
½ teaspoon salt

Method:

1. Soak salted vegetables in cold water for 20 minutes. Squeeze out excess water and chop coarsely.

2. Dice bean curd and drain.

3. Heat oil, stir-fry salted vegetables for 1 minute. Add soy sauce, sugar, salt, ¾ cup water and bean curd. Cook for 2 minutes or until bean curd is heated through.

Stir-fried
Bean Curd Balls

燒素肉圓

(Shao-su-jou-yüan)　Shanghai

Ingredients:

2 oz. (50 g) spinach, cut into 2-inch (6 cm) pieces
1 small carrot, cut crosswise into thin slices
1 tablespoon dried cloud ears
2 squares bean curd, about 3″ × 3″ (7.5 × 7.5 cm) each
¼ teaspoon salt
1 teaspoon flour
oil for deep-frying
2 teaspoons cornstarch dissolved in 2 tablespoons water
Mixture A:
　1½ tablespoons soy sauce
　1 teaspoon Chinese rice wine or sake
　1 teaspoon sugar
　1 cup chicken stock
　dash of MSG (optional)

Method:

1. Parboil carrot. Blanch spinach, then rinse with cold water and drain.

2. Soak cloud ears in hot water for 30 minutes, remove sand and rinse. Tear large ones into smaller pieces.

3. With a fork mash bean curd, mix in salt and flour. Form bean curd into small balls about ⅔ inch (2 cm) in diameter.

4. Heat oil, deep-fry bean curd balls over high heat until golden brown, drain. Remove all but 1 tablespoon oil from pan, add carrot and spinach, stir-fry for 30 seconds. Add cloud ears, bean curd balls and mixture A, bring to a boil. Thicken sauce with dissolved cornstarch.

Braised Bean Curd with
Pork

家常豆腐

(Chia-ch'ang-tou-fu)　Shanghai

Ingredients:

2 squares bean curd, about 3″ × 3″ (7.5 × 7.5 cm) each
1 tablespoon dried shrimp
1 tablespoon dried cloud ears
¼ lb. (125 g) lean pork
2 oz. (50 g) canned bamboo shoots
1 scallion, cut into 2-inch (6 cm) sections
1 chili pepper, seeded and chopped
7 tablespoons oil
Mixture A:
　2 tablespoons soy sauce
　1 teaspoon sugar
　1 tablespoon Chinese rice wine or sake
　½ cup chicken stock
　dash of MSG (optional)

Method:

1. In separate bowls, cover dried shrimp and cloud ears with hot water and soak for 30 minutes.

2. Cut bean curd into slices about ½ inch thick. Cut pork against the grain into very thin slices, and slice bamboo shoots into approximately the same shape as pork.

3. Heat 5 tablespoons oil, fry bean curd until golden brown, drain.

4. Heat the remaining 2 tablespoons oil until very hot. Add and stir-fry in sequence, scallion, dried shrimp, chili pepper and cloud ears, bring to a boil. Then reduce heat and simmer for 5 minutes.

Stuffed Deep-fried Bean Curd

扒豆腐盒

(Pa-tou-fu-ho) Tientsin

Ingredients:

2 pieces deep-fried bean curd
⅓ lb. (150 g) ground pork
2 tablespoons cornstarch
oil for deep-frying

Mixture A:
   2 teaspoons soy sauce
   2 teaspoons Chinese rice wine or sake
   2 tablespoons chicken stock
   1 tablespoon scallions
   1 teaspoon oil

Mixture B:
   1 teaspoon chopped scallions
   1 teaspoon minced fresh ginger
   2 tablespoons Chinese rice wine or sake
   2 tablespoons soy sauce
   2 tablespoons sugar
   dash of MSG (optional)
   1 cup chicken stock

Method:

1. Cut each deep-fried bean curd into 4 rectangles. Scoop out approximately 1 teaspoon of bean curd from cut surface of each piece to make a hole.

2. Mix ground pork with mixture A thoroughly. Stuff pork mixture into the holes, dredge each one with flour, then deep-fry them.

3. Heat 1 tablespoon oil in a skillet, add ginger and scallions, stir-fry for 30 seconds. Add wine, soy sauce, sugar, 1 cup stock and MSG. Simmer for 5 minutes. Place bean curd in sauce and cook for 1 more minute.

Shrimp and Deep-fried Bean Curd Soup

煮干絲

(Chu-kan-ssŭ) Hangchow

Ingredients:

1 large piece deep-fried bean curd
1 tablespoon oil
1 tablespoon minced scallions
5 cups chicken stock
1 tablespoon dried shrimp
pinch of salt
1 tablespoon Chinese rice wine or sake
dash of MSG (optional)
1 slice of cooked Smithfield ham, cut into thin slivers
1 teaspoon fresh ginger slivers

Method:

1. Place fried bean curd in bowl, pour boiling water over and soak for 10 minutes. By hand, squeeze the oil out of the fried bean curd. Cut into thin strips.

2. Heat oil, add scallion, stir-fry for 30 seconds, add chicken stock, dried shrimp, salt and wine. Simmer for 10 minutes. Add MSG.

3. Transfer soup to a large serving bowl and garnish with ham and ginger.

Sweet-and-Sour Wheat Gluten
溜面筋
(*Liu-mien-chin*) Shanghai

Ingredients:
¼ lb. (125 g) fried wheat gluten balls (*yu-mien-chin*)
1 large cabbage leaf
1 green pepper
1 tablespoon dried cloud ears
oil for deep-frying
Mixture A:
   2 tablespoons Chinese rice wine or sake
   2 tablespoons sugar
   2 tablespoons vinegar
   1½ tablespoons soy sauce
   ½ cup chicken stock or water
   1 teaspoon cornstarch

Method:
1. Cut cabbage leaf into 1½-inch (4 cm) squares. Cut green peppers from top to bottom, remove seeds and stems, then dice.

2. Soak cloud ears in hot water for 30 minutes. Tear large ones into smaller pieces.

3. Heat oil, when hot but not smoking, deep-fry wheat gluten balls for 30 seconds. Remove and drain.

4. Empty all but 2 tablespoons oil from pan, add cabbage, green peppers and cloud ears, stir-fry for 1 minute. Add mixture A and bring to a boil, then add wheat gluten balls and blend thoroughly.

Deep-fried Bean Curd Salad
青椒拌干絲
(*Ch'ing-chiao-pan-kan-ssŭ*) Suchow

Ingredients:
⅔ lb. (300 g) green peppers
1 large piece deep-fried bean curd
Mixture A:
   1 tablespoon sesame oil
   ½ teaspoon salt
   ½ tablespoon sugar
   dash of MSG (optional)

Method:
1. Cut green peppers from top to bottom in two, remove seeds and stems. Cut peppers into thin strips and parboil.

2. Place fried bean curd in a bowl, pour boiling water over and soak for 10 minutes. By hand, squeeze the oil out of the fried bean curd. Cut into thin strips.

3. Combine green peppers, fried bean curd and mixture A together and blend well.

Stir-fried Bean Curd Sticks

炒腐衣

(Ch'ao-fu-i) Shanghai

Ingredients:

¼ lb. (50 g) bok choi
2 oz. (50 g) canned bamboo shoots
1 teaspoon dried cloud ears
¼ lb. (125 g) dried bean curd sticks
3 tablespoons oil
Mixture A:
   1½ tablespoons soy sauce
   1 teaspoon sugar
   3 tablespoons Chinese rice wine or sake
   dash of MSG (optional)
1 teaspoon cornstarch dissolved in 1 tablespoon water

Method:

1. Parboil bok choi, cut into strips ½ inch (1.5 cm) wide by 2 inches (6 cm) long.

2. Cut bamboo shoots into thin slices 1 inch (3 cm) long by ½ inch (1.5 cm) wide.

3. Soak cloud ears in hot water for 30 minutes, tear large ones into smaller pieces.

4. Break bean curd sticks into 2-inch (6 cm) sections, then soak in lukewarm water for 20 minutes and drain.

5. Heat oil, add bok choi, bamboo shoots, cloud ears and bean curd sticks, stir-fry everything for 1 minute. Add mixture A and ½ cup water, cook for 1 minute. Thicken sauce with dissolved cornstarch and serve.

Sweet-and-Sour Bean Curd Sheets

滑面筋

(Hua-mien-chin) Tientsin

Ingredients:

¼ lb. (125 g) fresh bean curd sheets or fresh
   wheat gluten
oil for deep-frying
Mixture A:
   1 tablespoon soy sauce
   1 tablespoon vinegar
   2 tablespoons sugar
   ½ tablespoon Chinese rice wine or sake
   ¼ cup water
2 teaspoons cornstarch dissolved in 1 tablespoon water

Method:

1. With scissors cut bean curd sheet into 1-inch (3 cm) by 2-inch (6 cm) pieces.

2. Heat oil over high flame and fry bean curd sheets a small amount at a time until golden brown. Drain and place on a serving plate.

3. Empty all the oil from pan, add mixture A and dissolved cornstarch. Stir and bring to a boil, when sauce becomes thick, pour over fried bean curd sheets.

Note: In the original recipe wheat gluten is used instead of bean curd sheets.

Meats

Stir-fried Pork with Bean Sprouts

緑豆芽炒肉絲
(Lü-tou-ya-ch'ao-jou-ssŭ)   Suchow

Ingredients:
½ lb. (250 g) bean sprouts
¼ lb. (125 g) lean pork
½ egg white
1 teaspoon cornstarch
2 cups oil
½ teaspoon salt
Mixture A:
    1½ tablespoons sugar
    1½ tablespoons soy sauce
    1 tablespoon Chinese rice wine or sake

Method:

1. Rinse bean sprouts and drain.

2. Cut pork along the grain into thin slivers, mix with egg white and cornstarch.

3. Heat 2 cups oil to 210°F. over low heat, add pork and deep-fry until pinkish color is gone. With a strainer, remove pork from oil and drain.

4. Empty all but 2 tablespoons oil from pan, heat oil over high heat, then add salt and drop in bean sprouts. Stir-fry constantly for 30 seconds, add pork and mixture A, blend thoroughly. Transfer to plate and serve.

Note: Meat is more juicy and tender when it is cooked in a large amount of warm oil.

Do not overcook bean sprouts.

Beef or chicken cut into slivers, may be substituted for pork.

For a stronger flavor, add to step 4, green pepper strips or minced garlic, or scallions cut into 1-inch sections.

Stir-fried Pork with Onions

肉絲炒葱頭

(Jou-ssŭ-ch'ao-ts'ung-t'ou)　Peking

Ingredients:

¼ lb. (125 g) lean pork
2 medium onions
3 tablespoons oil
1 teaspoon minced fresh ginger
Mixture A:
　1 tablespoon soy sauce
　1 tablespoon brown bean paste
　½ teaspoon salt
　1 teaspoon sugar

Method:

1. Cut pork against the grain into slices ¼ inch (1 cm) thick, then cut into thin strips. Peel and cut onions lengthwise in half, then slice each half crosswise.

2. Heat oil until very hot, add ginger and cook for 30 seconds. Drop in pork, stir-fry until pinkish color is almost gone, add onions. Stir and cook until onions become soft. Add mixture A, blend well.

Note: For nice variations, substitute beef for pork, or shredded Chinese cabbage, or shredded giant white radish, or potatoes cooked with pork in the same way.

Stir-fried Pork with Ginger

炒姜絲肉

(Ch'ao-chiang-ssŭ-jou)　Shanghai

Ingredients:

½ lb. (250 g) lean pork
⅓ lb. (150 g) bean sprouts
1 green pepper
1 oz. (25 g) pickled ginger
4 tablespoons oil
Mixture A:
　1 tablespoon Chinese rice wine or sake
　1 tablespoon soy sauce
　1 teaspoon sugar
½ teaspoon salt
dash of MSG (optional)
2 teaspoons cornstarch dissolved in 2 tablespoons water

Method:

1. Cut pork against the grain into slices ¼ inch (1 cm) thick, then cut into thin strips.

2. Wash bean sprouts and drain.

3. Cut green pepper in half lengthwise, remove stems and seeds. Cut into strips. Cut ginger into thin slivers.

4. Heat 2 tablespoons oil over a medium fire, stir-fry pork for 1 minute, add mixture A. Remove from pan and set aside.

5. Heat 2 tablespoons oil, stir-fry ginger, green pepper and bean sprouts for 1 minute. Blend in salt, MSG and pork, then thicken with dissolved cornstarch.

51

Stir-fried Pork with Cabbage

炒肉片
(Ch'ao-jou-p'ien)   Peking

Ingredients:
6 oz. (200 g) pork, loin or fresh ham
1 scallion, cut into thin slivers
2 thin slices fresh ginger, cut into slivers
½ lb. (250 g) Chinese cabbage
2 tablespoons cloud ears
2 tablespoons oil
1 tablespoon Chinese rice wine or sake
2 tablespoons soy sauce
pinch of salt

Method:
1. Slice pork thin against the grain into 1-inch (3 cm) by 2-inch (6 cm) pieces.

2. Soak cloud ears in hot water for 30 minutes. Rinse well and tear large ones into small pieces.

3. Heat oil, add scallions and ginger, stir-fry for 30 seconds. Add pork and stir constantly until pinkish color is gone. Add wine, Chinese cabbage, cloud ears, soy sauce and salt. Stir and cook for 1 more minute or until cabbage becomes slightly soft.

Pork and Bean Curd Soup

肉絲豆腐羹

(Jou-ssŭ-tou-fu-kêng)　Suchow

Ingredients:

1½ squares bean curd, about 3″ × 3″ (7.5 × 7.5 cm) each

¼ lb. (125 g) canned bamboo shoots, sliced

⅓ lb. (150 g) pork, fresh ham or butt

1 tablespoon cloud ears

2 tablespoons oil

1 tablespoon Chinese rice wine or sake

3 cups chicken stock

1 teaspoon soy sauce

¼ teaspoon salt

dash of MSG (optional)

2 teaspoons cornstarch dissolved in 2 tablespoons water

15 snow peas, parboiled

Method:

1. Slice bean curd into 1½-inch (4 cm) squares, about ½ inch (1.5 cm) thick.

2. Cut pork into thin slices, about the same shape as bean curd.

3. Soak cloud ears in hot water for 30 minutes. Rinse well and cut into strips.

4. Heat oil over high flame, stir-fry pork for 30 seconds. Add wine, stock, soy sauce, bean curd, bamboo shoots and cloud ears. Bring to a rapid boil, then cover and simmer for 2 minutes. Add salt, MSG and dissolved cornstarch, bring soup to a boil again. Garnish with snow peas.

Stewed Pork with Chinese Cabbage

爛糊肉絲

(Lan-hu-jou-ssŭ)　Shanghai

Ingredients:

¼ lb. (125 g) lean pork

1⅔ lb. (750 g) Chinese cabbage

3 tablespoons oil

3 cups chicken stock

pinch of salt

dash of MSG (optional)

1 tablespoon cornstarch dissolved in 2 tablespoons water

Method:

1. Cut pork against the grain into slices ¼ inch (1 cm) thick, then cut into thin strips.

2. Wash cabbage and cut crosswise into sections 1 inch (3 cm) wide.

3. Heat 2 tablespoons oil until very hot, add pork and stir-fry until meat shows no sign of pink. Add wine and stock, bring to a boil. Drop in cabbage stems first then the leaves. Bring everyting to a rapid boil then reduce heat and simmer for 2 minutes.

4. Season with salt and MSG. Stir in dissolved cornstarch, and add 1 tablespoon oil.

Note: In step 1, pork may be marinated with 1 teaspoon cornstarch and ½ egg white. Then cook in 1 cup of oil until pinkish color is gone.

Sweet-and-Sour Pork

糖醋肉片
(T'ang-ts'u-jou-p'ien) Peking

Ingredients:
12 oz. (350 g) pork, loin or butt
½ cup cornstarch
2 cups oil for deep-frying
Mixture A:
  ¼ cup chicken stock or water
  2 tablespoons vinegar
  1 tablespoon Chinese rice wine or sake
  4 tablespoons sugar
  1 teaspoon salt
  1 teaspoon soy sauce
  1½ teaspoons cornstarch

Method:
1. Cut pork against the grain into ½-inch (1.5 cm) slices, then cut in 2-inch (6 cm) squares. Mix cornstarch with ½ cup water, coat pork with batter.

2. Heat oil, deep-fry pork until golden brown. Remove from oil and drain.

3. In a small bowl, combine mixture A.

4. Heat 1 tablespoon oil, add mixture A, stir and bring to a boil. Add pork and cook until sauce is thickened.

Note: When frying pork in order to cook the meat thoroughly, first heat oil over a high flame until very hot, then reduce heat when pork is added, and cook slowly until golden brown.

Stir-fried Pork with Eggplants
肉片燒茄子
(Jou-p'ien-shao-ch'ieh-tzŭ)   Shanghai

Ingredients:
1 lb. (500 g) eggplants
¼ lb. (125 g) pork, butt or fresh ham
1 scallion
1 teaspoon minced garlic
2 oz. (50 g) canned bamboo shoots
3 cups oil for deep-frying
1½ tablespoons soy sauce
1½ cups chicken stock
dash of MSG (optional)
2 teaspoons cornstarch dissolved in 1 tablespoon
   water
½ teaspoon sesame oil

Method:
1. Wash eggplants, cut unpeeled, from top to bottom into strips 1-inch (3 cm) thick. Cut each strip diagonally into 1-inch (3 cm) sections.

2. Cut pork against the grain into thin slices 1 inch (3 cm) by 2 inches (6 cm). Cut scallion into 1-inch (3 cm) sections. Slice bamboo shoots into same size as pork.

3. Heat oil, deep-fry eggplants for 1 minute, remove and drain. Empty all but 2 tablespoons oil from pan. Add scallion, garlic and pork, stir-fry for 1 minute over high heat. Add bamboo shoots, soy sauce, stock and MSG, bring to a boil, then simmer for 3 minutes over a low flame. Thicken sauce with dissolved cornstarch. Transfer to a plate and add sesame oil.

Stir-fried Pork with String Beans
肉片四季豆
(Jou-p'ien-ssŭ-chi-tou)   Suchow

Ingredients:
½ lb. (250 g) string beans
6 oz. (150 g) pork, loin or fresh ham
4 tablespoons oil
1½ tablespoons soy sauce
1 tablespoon Chinese rice wine or sake
1½ teaspoons sugar
½ teaspoon salt
¾ cup chicken stock or water

Method:
1. Rinse beans, snap off tips. Cut into 2-inch (6 cm) sections.

2. Slice pork thin against the grain then cut into 1-inch (3 cm) squares.

3. Heat 2 tablespoons oil until very hot, drop in pork and stir-fry for 1 minute. Add soy sauce, wine and sugar, stir and cook for another minute. Remove to plate and set aside.

4. Heat the remaining 2 tablespoons oil, when it is hot add beans, stir-fry beans for 1 minute, pour in stock, add salt. Cook until beans are tender. Drain off excess liquid. Return pork to pan with the beans and mix thoroughly.

55

Stir-fried Pork with Chili Pepper

辣子 肉 丁
(La-tzǔ-jou-ting)　Peking

Ingredients:

½ lb. (250 g) pork, loin or fresh ham
1 small cucumber
1 scallion, cut into ½-inch (1.5 cm) sections
1 chili pepper
1 tablespoon brown bean paste
1 teaspoon cornstarch
2 cups oil
1 teaspoon minced fresh ginger
pinch of salt
2 teaspoons Chinese rice wine or sake
1 teaspoon cornstarch dissolved in 1 tablespoon
　water

Method:

1. Dice pork, and mix with brown bean paste

and 1 teaspoon cornstarch.

2. Wash cucumber, and dice unpeeled.

3. Discard seeds from chili and chop.

4. Heat oil over medium heat, deep-fry and separate pork until pinkish color is gone. Remove from oil and drain.

5. Empty all but 2 tablespoons oil from pan, heat over high heat. Add ginger, scallion, chili pepper, cucumber, salt and 1 tablespoon chicken stock or water. Cook and stir all the ingredients for 1 minute. Add pork and wine, then thicken sauce with dissolved cornstarch.

Note:　Variations: for chili pepper use green pepper, or add diced bamboo shoots to step 5.

Stir-fried Pork with Bean Paste

醬 爆 肉 丁

(Chiang-pao-jou-ting)　Peking

Ingredients:

1 lb. (500 g) lean pork, loin or butt
½ egg white
1 teaspoon cornstarch
2 cups oil for deep-frying
Mixture A:
　2 tablespoons brown bean paste
　2 tablespoons sugar
　1½ tablespoons Chinese rice wine or sake
　½ teaspoon fresh ginger juice

Method:

1. Dice pork, and mix with egg white and cornstarch.

2. Heat oil until hot, about 210°F., drop in pork, stir and cook until pinkish color is gone. Remove and drain.

3. Empty all but 1 tablespoon oil from pan, heat over high flame. Add mixture A and bring to a boil, then add pork and blend well.

Note: While frying pork, watch closely to prevent browning the meat.

Do not boil mixture over very high heat; it will become bitter when overheated.

When using spinach to give color contrast to the dish, stir-fry spinach with 2 tablespoons oil, ½ teaspoon salt and ½ cup water. Then cover and simmer for 1 minute. Drain off excess liquid and place spinach either beneath or around the meat.

Stir-fried Pork with Scallions

葱 爆 肉 片

(Ts'ung-pao-jou-p'ien)　Shangtung

Ingredients:

½ lb. (250 g) pork, loin or fresh ham
2 scallions, cut into 1-inch (3 cm) sections
1 tablespoon cloud ears
3 tablespoons oil
3 tablespoons soy sauce
dash of MSG (optional)

Method:

1. Slice pork against the grain into pieces ¼ inch (1 cm) thick, then cut the slices into rectangles.

2. Soak cloud ears in hot water for 30 minutes. Rinse and tear large ones into small pieces.

3. Heat oil, stir-fry pork for about 1 minute. Add soy sauce, cloud ears, MSG and scallions. Stir and cook over high heat for 1–2 minutes.

Note: Rabbit meat, beef or lamb can be cooked in the same way.

Sweet-and-Sour Pork

糖 醋 咕 嚕 肉
(T'ang-ts'u-ku-lu-jou)   Canton

Ingredients:
1–2 chili peppers, seeded and chopped
1 scallion, cut into 2-inch (6 cm) sections
½ lb. (250 g) canned bamboo shoots
1 teaspoon minced garlic
1 lb. (500 g) pork, loin or fresh ham
pinch of salt
1 egg, beaten
½ cup cornstarch
oil for deep-frying
1 tablespoon cornstarch dissolved in 2 tablespoons water
Mixture A:
  ⅔ cup vinegar
  ⅔ cup sugar
  1 tablespoon ketchup
  1 teaspoon salt

Method:
1. Cut bamboo shoots into 1-inch (2.5 cm)
   wedges.

2. Score the surface of pork in diamond pattern,
   then cut into 2-inch (6 cm) squares about ½
   inch (1.5 cm) thick. Mix pork with salt and
   egg, then roll each piece in cornstarch.

3. Heat oil until merely warm, deep-fry pork
   over a medium fire until golden brown and
   crisp, remove from oil and drain. With the
   same oil, deep-fry bamboo shoots for 30
   seconds, drain.

4. In a small bowl combine mixture A.

5. Heat 1 tablespoon oil over high heat, stir-fry
   garlic and scallions for 30 seconds. Add chili
   and mixture A, bring to a boil, drop in pork
   and bamboo shoots, then thicken sauce with
   dissolved cornstarch. Blend thoroughly.

Note: Pork with some fat gives a more delicate
flavor. For color contrast, add cubed green pepper
and pineapple.

Steamed Pork in Lotus Leaves

荷葉粉蒸肉
(Ho-yeh-fên-chêng-jou)   Hangchow

Ingredients:

1 lb. (500 g) pork, fresh bacon
1 teaspoon minced fresh ginger
1 teaspoon minced scallions
¼ teaspoon five-spice powder (*wu-hsiang-fên,* page 13)
1 tablespoon rice powder
2–3 lotus leaves
Mixture A:
    4 tablespoons soy sauce
    3 tablespoons Chinese rice wine or sake
    2 tablespoons sugar
    ½ cup Sweet brown bean paste (*t'ien-mien-chiang,* page 14)

Method:

1. Rinse pork, cut into 10 even-sized rectangles. With a sharp knife, score each rectangle lengthwise, leaving about ½ inch (1.5 cm) uncut at bottom of score.

2. In a small bowl combine mixture A with ginger, scallions and five-spice powder. Marinate pork with the mixture for 30 minutes.

3. Toast rice powder in an ungreased pan over a low fire until light brown, then mix with pork.

4. Cut lotus leaves into 10 pieces, each piece big enough to wrap 1 portion of pork. Blanch lotus leaves. Wrap each portion of pork with one piece of leaf, then tie with string. Steam the packages for 2½ hours. Add water when needed.

Note: Pork is much more delicate when coated with flour and wrapped in lotus leaves. This method of cooking meat is quite common in China where many dishes are cooked in this fashion. If lotus leaves are unavailable substitute bamboo leaves, or just steam on a plate without wrappers.

    To reduce cooking time, cut pork into thinner pieces. This dish is convenient for picnics.

Braised Pork with Fermented Bean Curd
燉醬豆腐肉
(T'un-chiang-tou-fu-jou)　Peking

Ingredients:

1 lb. (500 g) pork, fresh bacon or fresh ham
1 scallion, chopped
1 tablespoon mashed red fermented bean curd
　(*hung-fu-ju*, page 12)
1 tablespoon oil
3 tablespoons Chinese rice wine or sake
4 tablespoons soy sauce
3 slices fresh ginger, about 1 inch (3 cm) in dia-
　meter each
3 tablespoons sugar

Method:

1. Cut pork into 1-inch (3 cm) cubes.

2. Heat oil over high heat until very hot, drop in pork and stir-fry until the pinkish color is gone.

3. Add wine, soy sauce, scallion, ginger, fermented red bean curd and sugar, stir-fry everything for 1 minute. Transfer to a pottery casserole, add 1 to 2 cups boiling water. Bring to a rapid boil, remove scum if any, cover and simmer for 1 hour.

Note: The word "*tun*" means to braise meat for long hours with seasonings and large amount of water.

Braised Spicy Pork
燉猪肉
(T'un-chu-jou)　Peking

Ingredients:

1 lb. (500 g) pork, butt or fresh bacon
½ scallion, cut into 1-inch (3 cm) sections
3 slices fresh ginger, about 1 inch (3 cm) in
　diameter each
1 tablespoon oil
1 tablespoon Chinese rice wine or sake
4 tablespoons soy sauce
1½ tablespoons sugar
1 star anise (see page 14)
½ stick cinnamon
chicken stock

Method:

1. Cut pork into 1-inch (3 cm) cubes.

2. Heat oil over high heat, stir-fry pork until pinkish color is gone. Add wine, soy sauce, sugar, scallion, ginger, star anise and cinnamon, stir and mix thoroughly.

3. Transfer to a pottery casserole, add stock, cover and simmer until meat is tender.

Steamed Pork with Eggs
元寶肉
(Yuan-pao-jou) Tientsin

Ingredients:
1 lb. (500 g) pork with skin, fresh bacon
oil for deep-frying
1 star anise
1 teaspoon minced fresh ginger
3 eggs
Mixture:
  3 tablespoons soy sauce
  3 tablespoons Chinese rice wine or sake
  ¼ teaspoon salt
  ¼ cup chicken stock
  1 tablespoon mashed red fermented bean curd
  (*hung-fu-ju*, page 12)

Method:
1. Boil the whole piece of pork in water for 10 minutes, or until about 70 percent cooked. Remove from water, pat dry with paper towels then brush with soy sauce.

2. Heat oil, and deep-fry pork until bubbles appear on the skin. Drain and cool for 10 minutes. Cut pork into large slices, about ¼ inch (7 mm) thick.

3. Put star anise and ginger in a bowl, place pork on top of the spices and pour in mixture A. Steam for 1½ hours.

4. Hardboil the eggs, discard shell and coat eggs with soy sauce. Deep-fry eggs until golden brown and cut each one lengthwise in half.

5. Place a plate on top of the bowl containing pork, invert plate and bowl together, then lift the bowl and leave moulded pork on plate. Arrange fried eggs and parsley around pork and serve.

Steamed Pork with Soy Sauce
紅燉肉
(Hung-t'un-jou) Suchow

Ingredients:
1 lb. (500 g) pork, butt or fresh ham
Mixture A:
  2 tablespoons Chinese rice wine or sake
  5 tablespoons soy sauce
  3 tablespoons sugar
  1 scallion, cut into 2-inch (6 cm) sections
  1 slice fresh ginger, about 1 inch (3 cm) in diameter

Method:
1. Cut pork into slices, about ¼ inch (7 mm) thick and 2 inches (6 cm) long.

2. Mix mixture A thoroughly and marinate pork for 2 hours.

3. Place pork and the marinade in a bowl. Cover bowl and steam for 3 hours. When pork is tender remove ginger and scallion. Invert the meat onto a plate and serve.

Braised Pork with Chestnuts
板栗燒肉
(Pan-li-shao-jou)   Chengtu

Ingredients:
⅔ lb. (300 g) chestnuts
1 lb. (500 g) pork, fresh bacon or butt
1 cup chicken stock
pinch of salt
4 tablespoons sugar
Mixture A:
  1 slice fresh ginger, about 1 inch (3 cm) in diameter
  1 scallion, cut into 2-inch (6 cm) sections
  ¼ cup Chinese rice wine or sake
  3 tablespoons soy sauce

Method:
1. With a sharp knife make a small cut through the skin of each chestnut. Cover chestnuts with water and boil for 1–2 minutes, remove from heat. Peel off shell and inner skin.

2. Cut pork into ⅔-inch (2 cm) cubes and blanch.

3. In a saucepan, cook pork and mixture A over high heat for 2 minutes. Add stock to cover meat, bring to a rapid boil. Cover pan, and simmer over a low fire for 20 minutes.

4. Add chestnuts and continue cooking. When chestnuts become tender, add salt and sugar. Remove scallions and ginger, then transfer meat and chestnuts to plate and serve.

Note: Stir occasionally to prevent sticking but use a light touch to avoid breaking the chestnuts.

Braised Pork and Radish
蘿蔔燒肉
(Lo-po-shao-jou)   Hankow

Ingredients:
1 lb. (500 g) pork, butt or fresh ham
⅔ lb. (300 g) giant white radish
1 scallion
3 tablespoons oil
1 slice fresh ginger, about 1 inch (3 cm) in diameter
2½ cups chicken stock
1½ tablespoons Chinese rice wine or sake
3 tablespoons soy sauce

¼ teaspoon salt
dash of MSG (optional)
2 teaspoons cornstarch dissolved in 1 tablespoon
  water
a few drops sesame oil

Method:

1. Cut pork into 1-inch (3 cm) squares about ½
   inch (1.5 cm) thick.

2. Peel and cut radish in half lengthwise, and
   slice diagonally into 1-inch (3 cm) wedges.

3. Cut scallion into slivers.

4. Heat oil, add ginger and pork, stir-fry for
   1 minute, then add wine. When pork is half
   cooked, add stock, bring to a rapid boil over
   high heat. Cover pan and simmer over low
   fire for 5 minutes.

5. Drop in radish, add soy sauce, scallions and
   salt. Cover and cook over low heat for 10
   more minutes.

6. Turn heat to high, boil pork and radish for 2
   more minutes. Add MSG then thicken sauce
   with dissolved cornstarch. Sprinkle a few
   drops of sesame oil just before serving.

Note: This dish may be cooked several hours ahead
of time and reheated before serving.

Pork with Bean Paste

醬爆肉

(Chiang-pao-jou) Chungking

Ingredients:

1 lb. (500 g) lean pork
3 tablespoons oil
1 tablespoon sweet bean paste (*t'ien-mien-chiang*,
  page 14)
1 tablespoon soy sauce
1 tablespoon chopped scallions
1 teaspoon sugar

Method:

1. Rinse pork, cover with water and simmer for
   20 minutes. Cut pork into thin slices, about
   1 inch (3 cm) by 2 inches (6 cm).

2. Heat oil, and stir-fry pork over high heat for
   1 minute. Add sweet bean paste, soy sauce
   and scallions, stir and cook for 1 more minute.
   Add sugar and blend thoroughly.

Note: In this recipe scallion is substituted for
garlic leaves. In step 2, minced garlic, minced fresh
ginger and scallion may be added and stir-fried before the pork.

Steamed Pork with Bean Curd

葷素扣肉
(Hsün-su-k'ou-jou) Peking

Ingredients:
½ lb. (250 g) pork, fresh ham or butt
1 scallion, cut into thin slivers
1 piece fresh ginger, about 1 inch (3 cm) in diameter, cut into thin slivers
1 cup plus 1 tablespoon soy sauce
4–5 tablespoons oil
1 square bean curd, about 3″ × 3″ (7.5 × 7.5 cm)
pinch of salt

Method:
1. Boil whole piece of pork in water for 5 minutes or until about 70 percent cooked.

2. Place pork in a small saucepan, add 1 cup soy sauce, and simmer over a medium fire until pork is well coated with soy sauce. Turn the meat over a few times for even cooking, remove and cool.

3. Heat oil until hot, and brown both sides of pork. Drain and cool, then cut pork into slices ¼ inch (7 mm) thick.

4. Cut bean curd into slices ¼ inch (7 mm) thick and deep-fry until golden brown, drain.

5. Place in a bowl alternately overlapping 1 piece of pork and 1 piece of bean curd. Spread ginger and scallions over, then add 1 tablespoon soy sauce, pinch of salt and 1 cup water.

6. Steam pork for 15 minutes. Place a plate on top of the bowl containing pork, invert plate and bowl together, then lift the bowl, leaving moulded pork on plate.

Note: Cooked green vegetables may be placed around the pork.

Braised Pork with Dractvegetable

干菜燒肉

(Kan-ts'ai-shao-jou)   Shanghai

Ingredients:

1 lb. (500 g) pork, butt or fresh ham
1 scallion, cut into 2-inch (6 cm) sections
2 slices fresh ginger, about 1 inch (3 cm) in diameter, crushed
1 tablespoon sugar
2 oz. (40 g) dried vegetables (*kan-ts'ai*,
   page 9)
1 tablespoon soy sauce
Mixture A:
   2 tablespoons Chinese rice wine or sake
   2 tablespoons sugar
   4 tablespoons soy sauce

Method:

1. Cut pork into 1-inch (3 cm) cubes, cover with
   5 cups of water and boil for 5 minutes. Remove pork and set aside liquid.

2. Place pork in a pottery casserole, add ginger,
   scallion, mixture A and 3 cups fresh water.
   Bring to a rapid boil over high heat, then
   cover pan and simmer for 1 hour over a low
   fire. After simmering turn heat to high and
   boil vigorously to evaporate most of the liquid. Place pork and sauce in a bowl.

3. Soak dried vegetables in lukewarm water for
   15 minutes. Rinse well and cut crosswise into
   pieces ½ inch (1.5 cm) wide.

4. Put dried vegetables in the liquid set aside in
   step one, add 1 tablespoon soy sauce and 1
   tablespoon sugar, then simmer for 20 minutes. Drain. Place dried vegetables on top of
   the pork in the same bowl.

5. Just before serving, cover bowl with a plate
   and steam for 15 minutes. Invert plate and
   bowl together, then lift up bowl, leaving pork
   and vegetables on plate.

Stewed Pork with Onion

剝皮大烤

(Po-p'i-ta-kao)   Hangchow

Ingredients:

½ lb. (250 g) pork, fresh ham
2 oz. (50 g) onion
2 tablespoons oil
2 tablespoons mashed red fermented bean curd
   (*hung-fu-ju*, page 12)
2 tablespoons Chinese rice wine or sake
2 tablespoons sugar
⅔ lb. (300 g) spinach or any green vegetables
   (more or less, according to taste) blanched

Method:

1. Cut pork into strips, about ⅓ inch (7 mm)
   thick and 1½ inches (4 cm) long. Blanch.

2. Cut onion into thin strips.

3. Heat oil, stir-fry onion and pork together for
   1 minute. Add fermented bean curd, wine and
   sugar, bring to a boil then simmer over a low
   fire for 20–30 minutes.

4. Put blanched spinach on a plate and place
   pork on top.

Note: Fermented bean curd adds delicate taste to
a dish but it is very salty and one should not use too
much.

Boiled Pork
白切肉
(Pai-ch'ieh-jou) Suchow

Ingredients:

1 lb. (500 g) pork, loin or fresh ham
1 slice fresh ginger, about 1½ inches (4.5 cm) in
  diameter
½ scallion, chopped
2 tablespoons Chinese rice wine or sake
1 teaspoon salt
3 tablespoons shrimp sauce (see page 15)
1 teaspoon minced garlic

Method:

1. Cover pork with water, bring to a boil and
   remove scum if any. Add ginger, scallion and
   wine, cook over low heat for 1 hour.

2. Remove pork from pan, place on plate with
   fat side down and sprinkle with salt. Cool
   thoroughly.

3. In a small bowl combine shrimp sauce and
   garlic.

4. Cut pork into thin slices, transfer to plate,
   pour shrimp sauce mixture over and serve.

Note: This dish is easy to prepare and also a nice
dish for summer.
   For variations, add mustard, or ground sesame
seeds to the sauce, or substitute soy sauce and
vinegar mixture for shrimp sauce.

Boiled Pork with Mung Bean Noodles
粉皮涼拌白肉
(Fên-p'i-liang-pan-pai-jou) Hankow

Ingredients:

1 lb. (500 g) lean pork, loin or fresh ham
2 oz. (50 g) dried mung bean noodles
1 tablespoon sesame oil
1 teaspoon minced garlic
1 tablespoon mustard
1½ tablespoons vinegar
1 tablespoon sesame paste (*chi-ma-chiang*,
  page 14)
Mixture A:
  1½ tablespoons soy sauce
  1 teaspoon vinegar
  1½ tablespoons sugar
  1 tablespoon sesame oil

Method:

1. Cut pork along the grain into 3 portions, then
   boil until no pinkish juice comes out when
   poked with a skewer. Remove from pan and
   cool.

2. Cut pork into thin slices, about 1 inch (3 cm)
   long by ⅔ inch (2 cm) wide. Mix pork with
   mixture A and set aside.

3. Boil mung bean noodles in water for 1 minute, drain and mix in 1 tablespoon sesame oil.
   Let cool thoroughly.

4. In a small bowl, combine garlic, mustard and
   vinegar. Put sesame paste in another small
   bowl.

5. Place noodles on a plate, arrange pork neatly
   on noodles. Serve with mustard sauce mixture
   and sesame paste.

Twice Cooked Pork

回 鍋 肉

(Hui-kuo-jou)　Tsingtao

Ingredients:

1 lb. (500 g) pork, loin or fresh ham
2 oz. (50 g) canned bamboo shoots
1 scallion, cut into 1-inch (3 cm) sections
1 chili, seeded and cut into ⅓-inch (1 cm) pieces
3 tablespoons oil
1 tablespoon sweet bean paste (*t'ien-mien-chiang*, page 14)
2 tablespoons Chinese rice wine or sake
1½ tablespoons sugar
3 tablespoons soy sauce
1 teaspoon dried cloud ears, soaked
⅓ cup chicken stock
sesame oil

Method:

1. Cover pork with water, bring to a boil, then simmer for 30 minutes. Drain and let meat cool. Cut into thin slices 2½ inches (7 cm) long by 1½ inches (4 cm) wide.

2. Cut bamboo shoots into slices about 1 inch (1.5 cm) long by ½ inch (1.5 cm) wide.

3. Heat oil, add garlic, scallion and bamboo shoots, stir-fry for 30 seconds. Add sweet bean paste, wine, sugar, soy sauce, pork, cloud ears and stock. Cook and stir until liquid is evaporated, sprinkle with sesame oil.

Stir-fried Pork with Eggs (Mu-shu-pork)

炒 木 須 肉

(Ch'ao-mu-hsü-jou)　Peking

Ingredients:

¼ lb. (125 g) pork, butt, loin or fresh ham
3 eggs, beaten
5 tablespoons oil
1 scallion, cut into slivers
1 tablespoon chicken stock
Mixture A:
　1 tablespoon soy sauce
　1 tablespoon Chinese rice wine or sake
　1 teaspoon fresh ginger juice
　pinch of salt

Method:

1. Cut pork into thin strips, about 2 inches (6 cm) long.

2. Heat 3 tablespoons oil, pour in eggs and scramble in hot oil until set. Remove to plate.

3. Heat the remaining 2 tablespoons oil, add pork and scallions, stir-fry for 1 minute. Add mixture A, eggs and stock, cook and stir for 1 more minute.

Note:　Ground pork may be used in place of sliced pork.

Stewed Meatballs with Chinese Cabbage

清燉獅子頭
(*Ch'ing-tun-shih-tzŭ-t'ou*)　Hangchow

Ingredients:
1 lb. (500 g) ground pork
2/3 lb. (300 g) Chinese cabbage
3 cups chicken stock
Mixture A:
　1 egg white
　1 teaspoon Chinese rice wine or sake
　1 teaspoon salt
　1 tablespoon cornstarch

Method:
1. Pound pork with the blunt side of a cleaver until meat becomes sticky.
2. In a bowl, mix meat with mixture A.
3. Divide meat mixture into 10 portions and form into meatballs. (If meat sticks to hands grease hands with oil.)
4. Rinse Chinese cabbage, and cut crosswise into 2-inch (6 cm) sections.
5. Bring stock to a boil in a pottery casserole, put in one half of the cabbage, place meatballs on top, then cover meatballs with the remaining cabbage. Cover, and simmer over low heat for 40–60 minutes until most of the liquid is evaporated.

Note: The name of this dish *shih-tzu-t'ou* means "lion head." The pork balls are said to represent the heads of lions and the cabbage serves as the manes.

Stewed Meatballs with Potatoes

葷素獅子頭
(*Hsün-su-shih-tzŭ-t'ou*)　Shanghai

Ingredients:
1/2 lb. (250 g) potatoes
1/2 lb. (250 g) ground pork
oil for deep-frying
1 lb. (500 g) green vegetables (spinach or leaf lettuce)
2 tablespoons soy sauce
1 cup chicken stock
Mixture A:
　1 egg
　1 tablespoon soy sauce
　2 tablespoons cornstarch
　1 teaspoon Chinese rice wine or sake

Method:
1. Peel and boil potatoes, then mash. Set aside to cool.
2. Pound ground pork with the blunt side of a cleaver. Mix pork with potatoes and mixture A.
3. Divide pork mixture into 4 portions and form into large balls.
4. Heat oil, and deep-fry potato meatballs over a moderate fire until golden brown, drain.
5. Wash vegetables, then cut long pieces crosswise into 2-inch (6 cm) sections.
6. In a saucepan, bring soy sauce and stock to a boil, add meatballs. Cover and simmer over low fire for 20 minutes.
7. Stir-fry vegetables in 2 tablespoons oil, then add to the meatballs and simmer 2 minutes.

Pearl Balls

蒸糯米圓子

(Chêng-no-mi-yüan-tzŭ)   Hankow

Ingredients:
1 cup glutinous rice
¾ lb. (350 g) ground pork
¼ lb. (125 g) water chestnuts
Mixture A:
  1 teaspoon salt
  1 egg
  1 tablespoon minced scallions
  1 teaspoon minced fresh ginger
  1 tablespoon Chinese rice wine or sake
  1 tablespoon cornstarch
  dash of MSG (optional)
  dash of pepper

Method:
1. Soak glutinous rice overnight and drain.

2. Pound pork with a meat hammer or the blunt side of a cleaver. Peel water chestnuts and cut into pea-sized pieces.

3. Mix pork with mixture A and 1 tablespoon water. Blend thoroughly by hand.

4. Add water chestnuts to pork mixture, then form into small meatballs, about 1 inch (3 cm) in diameter.

5. Roll meatballs in glutinous rice and steam for 15 minutes over high heat.

Note: Bamboo shoots may be substituted for water chestnuts.

Braised Meatballs

南煎丸子

(Nan-chien-wan-tzŭ)   Peking

Ingredients:
⅔ lb. (300 g) ground pork
1 egg, beaten
½ cup oil
1 tablespoon Chinese wine or sake
1¼ cups chicken stock or water
1 tablespoon soy sauce
1 teaspoon cornstarch dissolved in 1 tablespoon water
Mixture A:
  ½ tablespoon brown bean paste
  1 teaspoon minced scallions
  1 teaspoon minced fresh ginger
  pinch of salt
  1 tablespoon cornstarch

Method:
1. Pound pork with the blunt side of a cleaver.

2. In a bowl, mix pork with egg and mixture A, then form the whole thing into 1 large ball.

3. Heat oil, put in meatball, with a spatula flatten the ball and make it into a pancake-like shape. Fry until the bottom side becomes brown, drain off excess oil in pan, turn the meatball over and brown the other side. Reduce heat and cook over low heat until the meat is thoroughly cooked.

4. Add wine, stock and soy sauce, and continue to simmer until half of the liquid is left in the pan. Thicken with dissolved cornstarch.

Note: Since the meatball is rather big, be sure to cook thoroughly.

Sweet-and-sour Meatballs

溜丸子
(Liu-wan-tzǔ)   Peking

Ingredients:
⅔ lb. (300 g) ground pork
1 tablespoon cornstarch
1½ tablespoons brown bean paste
1 teaspoon minced fresh ginger
oil for deep-frying
1 tablespoon slivered scallions
1 teaspoon minced garlic
Mixture A:
   ½ cup chicken stock or water
   2 teaspoons Chinese rice wine or sake
   3 tablespoons soy sauce
   2 tablespoons vinegar
   1½ tablespoons cornstarch

Method:
1. Pound pork with the blunt side of a Chinese cleaver. Mix pork with 1 tablespoon cornstarch, bean paste and ginger.

2. Divide pork mixture into 30 portions and form into meatballs.

3. Heat large amount of oil, deep-fry meatballs over high heat until they turn slightly brown, then lower heat and fry until golden brown.

4. In a small bowl combine mixture A.

5. Heat 3 tablespoons oil, stir-fry scallions and garlic for 30 seconds. Add mixture A, and bring to a boil, then add meatballs.

Note: Since brown bean paste is already mixed in with the pork, the amount of soy in the sweet-and-sour sauce should be regulated according to taste.

   When green peppers and pineapple are added, this dish tastes just like sweet-and-sour pork.

Stuffed Cucumber

黄 瓜 塞 肉
(Huang-kua-sai-jou)　Hangchow

Ingredients:
2 medium cucumbers
¼ lb. (125 g) ground pork
oil for deep-frying
cornstarch for dusting
½ tablespoon cornstarch dissolved in 1 table-
　spoon water
a few drops of sesame oil
Mixture A:
　1 teaspoon Chinese rice wine or sake
　1½ teaspoons soy sauce
　½ tablespoon sugar
　dash of MSG (optional)
Mixture B:
　2 tablespoons Chinese rice wine or sake
　3 tablespoons soy sauce
　¼ teaspoon salt
　1½ tablespoons sugar

dash of MSG (optional)
1 cup chicken stock

Method:
1. Peel and cut cucumbers crosswise into 1½-
　inch (4.5 cm) sections, scoop out and discard
　seeds.

2. Pound ground pork with a meat hammer or
　the blunt side of a Chinese cleaver. Mix meat
　and mixture A thoroughly, stuff meat mixture
　into cucumbers, then dust both ends with
　cornstarch. Deep-fry over medium heat for
　about 3 minutes.

3. Place cucumbers in a pan, add mixture B and
　simmer over a moderate fire until most of the
　liquid has evaporated. Thicken sauce with
　dissolved cornstarch and add sesame oil.

Stir-fried Ground Pork Celery
肉末炒芹菜
(Jou-mo-ch'ao-ch'in-ts'ai) Peking

Ingredients:
1 lb. (500 g) celery
1 tablespoon oil
1 tablespoon chopped scallions
1 teaspoon minced fresh ginger
½ lb. (125 g) ground pork
1 teaspoon brown bean paste, ground
1 tablespoon soy sauce
pinch of salt

Method:
1. Rinse celery, remove and discard leaves. Dice the stalks and blanch. Drain and set aside.

2. Heat oil, add scallion and ginger, stir-fry for 30 seconds. Add pork, stir and cook over high heat for 1 minute. When pinkish color is almost gone, add bean paste, soy sauce and celery. Stir-fry for 1 minute then add salt and blend thoroughly.

Note: To enhance the flavor, add 1 teaspoon sugar and ½ teaspoon sesame oil to the sauce.
Do not overcook celery.

Pork with Taro
骨醬芋艿
(Ku-chiang-yü-nai) Shanghai

Ingredients:
1 lb. (500 g) pork loin
½ lb. (250 g) taro root
2 tablespoons Chinese rice wine or sake
4½ tablespoons soy sauce
1½ tablespoons sugar
1 tablespoon chopped scallions
1 teaspoon minced fresh ginger
1 cup chicken stock
dash of MSG (optional)
½ tablespoon cornstarch dissolved in 1 table-spoon water

Method:
1. Cut pork into pieces ⅔ inch (2 cm) wide by 2 inches (6 cm) long.

2. Peel and boil taro for 10 minutes.

3. Heat oil, stir-fry for 1 minute. Add 1 tablespoon wine, 1½ tablespoons soy sauce, 1½ tablespoons sugar, ginger, scallions and 1½ cups water, stir pork a few times, then cover and simmer for 30 minutes, cook until there is only ½ cup of liquid in the pan.

4. Turn heat to high, add taro, 1 cup stock, 1 tablespoon wine, 3 tablespoons soy sauce and MSG, then thicken sauce with dissolved cornstarch.

Pork Chop with Curry
咖喱猪排
(Ka-li-chu-p'ai) Hangchow

Ingredients:
2–3 scallions
1½ lb. (750 g) pork chops
pinch of salt
1 teaspoon Chinese rice wine or sake
dash of MSG (optional)
flour for dusting
2 tablespoons oil
1½ tablespoons curry powder

Method:
1. Cut scallions into 1-inch (3 cm) sections.

2. Buy thin pork chops, about ½ inch (1.5 cm) thick. Pound both sides with a meat hammer, then cut into 1-inch (3 cm) by 2-inch (6 cm) pieces.

3. Sprinkle pork with salt, then mix with wine and MSG. Dust each piece with flour.

4. In a skillet heat oil and brown both sides of chops slightly. Remove to plate, empty all but 1 tablespoon oil from pan, add scallions and stir-fry for 30 seconds. Add curry powder, ½ cup water, ½ teaspoon salt and MSG, place meat in curry sauce and simmer for 2 minutes.

Note: ½ tablespoon soy sauce may be added to the sauce.

Sparerib Soup
排骨湯
(P'ai-ku-t'ang) Hankow

Ingredients:
½ lb. (250 g) spareribs or loin
oil for deep-frying
1 slice fresh ginger, about 1 inch (3 cm) in diameter
½ teaspoon Chinese rice wine or sake
1 tablespoon slivered scallions
dash of MSG

Method:
1. Cut spareribs or loin into pieces 1 inch (3 cm) wide by 1½ inches (4 cm) long.

2. Heat oil and deep-fry spareribs for 10 minutes.

3. Place spareribs, ginger, salt, wine and 8 cups of water in a pottery casserole. Bring everything to a boil over high heat, then simmer over low heat for 2 hours.

4. Add scallions and MSG, simmer for 30 more minutes.

Note: Always remove scum if any.

Stir-fried Pork Liver

炒 猪 肝

(Ch'ao-chu-kan)   Suchow

Ingredients:

½ lb. (250 g) pork liver
pinch of salt
¼ lb. (125 g) canned bamboo shoots
1 scallion, cut into 1-inch (3 cm) sections
1 tablespoon cornstarch
oil for deep-frying
3 tablespoons chicken stock
2 teaspoons cornstarch dissolved in 1 tablespoon
   water
a few drops of sesame oil
Mixture A:
   1 tablespoon Chinese rice wine or sake
   1½ tablespoons soy sauce
   1 tablespoon sugar

Method:

1. Rinse liver under running water, slice paper-thin and mix with salt.

2. Slice bamboo shoots into thin pieces.

3. Coat liver with 1 tablespoon cornstarch, and deep-fry in oil over a moderate fire for 1 minute. Remove and drain.

4. Empty all but 1 tablespoon of oil from pan, stir-fry scallions and bamboo shoots for 30 seconds. Add liver, mixture A and stock, bring to a boil then thicken sauce with dissolved cornstarch. Sprinkle with sesame oil and serve.

Stir-fried Liver with Pickled Mustard Greens

咸 菜 猪 肝

(Hsien-ts'ai-chu-kan)   Shanghai

Ingredients:

¼ lb. (125 g) pickled mustard greens (red-in-snow, page 9)
⅔ lb. (350 g) pork liver
4½ tablespoons oil
1¾ cups chicken stock
1 tablespoon cornstarch dissolved in 2 table-spoons water
Mixture A:
   1 teaspoon Chinese rice wine or sake
   1 tablespoon soy sauce
   ⅓ teaspoon sugar
   dash of MSG (optional)

Method:

1. Soak pickled mustard greens for 15 minutes. Remove excess water and chop.

2. Rinse liver under running water and cut into very thin pieces about 2 inches (5 cm) long and ½ inch (1.5 cm) wide. Rinse the liver slices thoroughly and drain.

3. Heat 2 tablespoons oil and stir-fry pickled vegetables for 1 minute, remove from pan and set aside.

4. With paper towels, wipe off the remaining oil in the pan. Add 2½ tablespoons oil to pan and stir-fry liver over high heat for 1 minute. Stir in mixture A and add stock then the pickled vegetables. Bring the ingredients to a rapid boil and thicken with dissolved cornstarch.

Stir-fried Pork Kidney with Bean Curd

腰丁烩腐皮

(Yao-ting-hui-fu-p'i)   Hangchow

Ingredients:

1 pork kidney
2 bean curd sticks
2 tablespoons oil
1 tablespoon chopped scallions
1 tablespoon Chinese rice wine or sake
pinch of salt
dash of MSG (optional)
¼ cup chicken stock
½ tablespoon cornstarch dissolved in 1 tablespoon water

Method:

1. Cut kidney in half lengthwise, cut away fat and remove tough white veins. Score the surface of each half diagonally in crisscross pattern, then dice.

2. Parboil kidney for 1 minute and drain.

3. Break bean curd sticks crosswise into ½-inch (1.5 cm) sections. Soak in water for 20 minutes, drain and squeeze by hand to remove excess water.

4. Heat oil, stir-fry scallions for 20 seconds, add wine, salt, MSG and bean curd sticks. Bring sauce to a boil, add kidney then thicken sauce with dissolved cornstarch.

Fried Pork Kidney

軟炸腰花

(Juan-cha-yao-hua)   Hangchow

Ingredients:

1 pork kidney
1 egg, beaten
½ tablespoon Chinese rice wine or sake
pinch of salt
flour
oil for deep-frying
Szechuan peppercorn salt (*hua-chaio-yen*, page 15)
sweet bean paste (*t'ien-mien-chiang*, page 14)

Method:

1. Cut kidney in half lengthwise, cut away fat and remove tough white veins. Make a few cuts lengthwise in the center of each kidney, then cut crosswise into thin slices.

2. Mix egg with wine, salt, flour and 1 tablespoon water to make a batter.

3. Coat kidney with egg batter and deep-fry kidney in oil over moderate fire until crisp. Drain.

4. With a strainer, remove pieces of batter that are floating on top of the oil. Turn heat to high, return fried kidney to oil and fry until light brown. Drain.

5. Place kidney on a plate lined with leaf lettuce. Serve with Szechuan peppercorn salt or *t'ien-mien-chiang*.

Stir-fried Salt Pork

生爆鹽煎肉

(Shêng-pao-yen-chien-jou)　Chengtu

Ingredients:

1 lb. (500 g) salt pork
2 scallions, cut into 2-inch (6 cm) sections
1 tablespoon ground brown bean paste
3 tablespoons oil
1 tablespoon fermented black beans, crushed (see page 13)
1 tablespoon sweet bean paste (*t'ien-mien-chiang*, page 14)
3 tablespoons soy sauce

Method:

1. Cut salt pork into thin slices about 2 inches (6 cm) long and 1 inch (3 cm) wide.

2. Heat oil over high heat, stir-fry scallions for 5 seconds, add salt pork, fermented black beans, brown bean paste and sweet bean paste. Stir and cook for 1 minute, add soy sauce and mix thoroughly.

Note:　This dish is a bit salty, and is excellent for serving with cooked plain rice. Scallions have been substituted for garlic leaves.

When garlic leaves are available, add before soy sauce in step 2.

Homemade salt pork is made by adding 1 tablespoon salt to 1 pound of pork, rub salt over meat and wrap tightly with a piece of plastic, then keep in refrigerator for a day or two.

Since salt pork will keep for a long time, make a large amount ahead of time.

Salt Pork with Bamboo Shoots

南肉竹笋

(Nan-jou-chu-sun)　Hangchow

Ingredients:

⅓ lb. (500 g) salt pork
¼ lb. (125 g) canned bamboo shoots
3 cups chicken stock
1 tablespoon Chinese rice wine or sake
1 teaspoon salt
dash of MSG (optional)

Method:

1. Cut salt pork and bamboo shoots into slices 1-inch (3 cm) square and 1 inch (3 cm) thick.

2. Simmer pork and bamboo shoots in stock until pork is tender. Add wine, salt and MSG.

Note:　Add soy sauce and sugar to enhance the flavor, but cut down the amount of salt or omit it.

Fried Pig Intestines

干炸肥腸

(*Kan-cha-fei-ch'ang*)   Hangchow

Ingredients:

½ lb. (250 g) pig intestines
1 scallion
1 slice fresh ginger, about 1 inch in diameter
½ tablespoon Chinese rice wine or sake
½ tablespoon soy sauce
oil for deep-frying
½ tablespoon Szechuan peppercorn salt (*hua-chiao-yen*, page 15)
sweet bean paste (*t'ien-mien-chiang*, page 14)
1 medium onion, sliced

Method:

1. Wash pig intestines in hot water, remove and discard white fat. Rinse thoroughly with cold water.

2. Place intestines in a pan and cover with water. Add ginger, scallion and wine, then cover and cook over a moderate fire for 30 minutes. Remove from water and drain. Coat the intestines with soy sauce while still hot.

3. Heat oil over high heat and deep-fry the intestines until crisp and golden brown. Remove from oil and drain.

4. With a pair of scissors, cut fried intestines into 2-inch (6 cm) sections. Insert a strip of onion into each section and put the remaining onion on a plate, then place the intestines on top of the onion. Serve with Szechuan peppercorn salt and/or sweet bean paste.

Pork Stomach Soup (Pig Tripe Soup)

清燉肚子湯

(*Ch'ing-tun-tu-tzu-t'ang*)   Hankow

Ingredients:

½ lb. (250 g) pork stomach (pork tripe)
salt
½ scallion
1 slice of fresh ginger
2 tablespoons oil
dash of MSG (optional)

Method:

1. Remove and discard the fat on the surface of tripe. Turn the tripe inside out, rub vigorously with large amount of salt, then rinse thoroughly with water. If the inner lining of tripe is still slippery, repeat process of rubbing with salt and rinsing with water. Cover tripe with water and boil for 30 minutes. Discard water and rinse tripe thoroughly.

2. Cut prepared tripe into strips 1 inch (3 cm) long and ⅓ inch (1 cm) wide.

3. Chop scallion coarsely and crush the ginger.

4. Heat oil over medium heat, stir-fry scallion and ginger for 15 seconds, add tripe. Cook and stir for about 8 minutes, then mix in 1 teaspoon salt.

5. Transfer everything to a pottery casserole and add 6 cups of water. Cover and simmer for 2 hours. Season with salt and MSG before serving.

Braised Beef

煨牛肉

(Wei-niu-jou) Peking

Ingredients:

1 lb. (500 g) beef shank
1 scallion, coarsely chopped
oil for deep-frying
1 teaspoon Szechuan peppercorns
1 star anise
1 2-inch stick cinnamon
2 slices fresh ginger, about 1 inch (3 cm) in diameter each
2 tablespoons sugar
4 tablespoons soy sauce

Method:

1. Cut beef into 1½-inch (4 cm) cubes.

2. Heat oil over high flame and deep-fry beef until light brown.

3. Wrap Szechuan peppercorns, star anise and cinnamon stick with a piece of cheesecloth and tie with string.

4. Pour 3 cups of water into a pottery casserole, add the spice bag, scallion, ginger, sugar, soy sauce and beef. Place a plate on top of the meat to weigh it down. Cover pan and simmer for about 2 hours.

Stewed Beef with Tomatoes

西紅柿黃燜牛肉

(Hsi-hung-shih-huang-mên-niu-jou) Tientsin

Ingredients:

1 lb. (500 g) beef shank

2 scallions, chopped
2 slices fresh ginger, about 1 inch (3 cm) in diameter each
1 star anise
½ lb. (250 g) tomatoes
5 tablespoons sugar
oil for deep-frying
1½ tablespoons cornstarch dissolved in 2 tablespoons water
Szechuan peppercorn oil (see page 15)
Mixture A:
  1½ tablespoons soy sauce
  2½ tablespoons sugar
  ½ tablespoon Chinese rice wine or sake
  dash of MSG (optional)
  1¼ cups stock

Method:

1. Place the whole piece of beef without cutting in a heavy saucepan. Cover beef with water, add 1 slice of ginger, half of a star anise and half of the scallions, cover and simmer for 2–3 hours.

2. Blanch tomatoes, peel and dice. In a small pan, cook tomatoes with 5 tablespoons of sugar for 2 minutes and set aside.

3. Cube the cooked beef then deep-fry in hot oil over high heat for 1 minute, remove and drain.

4. Empty all but 2 tablespoons oil from pan, add the remaining half of the star anise and cook until slightly burned. Add the other slice of ginger, the remaining scallions and mixture A, cook for 30 seconds, add beef and simmer for 5 minutes. Last, stir in tomatoes, simmer for 2 more minutes. Thicken sauce with dissolved cornstarch and sprinkle with Szechuan peppercorn oil.

Stir-fried Lamb with Scallions
葱爆羊肉片
(Ts'ung-pao-yang-jou-p'ien)　Hangchow

Ingredients:
1 lb. (500 g) lamb
2 scallions
2 cloves garlic
1 tablespoon cornstarch
oil for deep-frying
1 teaspoon sesame oil
Mixture A:
　2 tablespoons soy sauce
　1 tablespoon Chinese rice wine or sake
　½ teaspoon salt

Method:
1. Cut lamb into very thin slices 2 inches (6 cm) by 3 inches (9 cm) in size.

2. Cut scallions into slivers. Crush garlic.

3. In a bowl mix lamb with cornstarch and 1 tablespoon water. Heat oil over high flame and deep-fry lamb until light brown. Drain.

4. Empty all but 2 tablespoons oil from pan, add scallions and garlic, stir-fry for 30 seconds, add lamb and stir in mixture A. Mix everything thoroughly and sprinkle with sesame oil.

Braised Lamb
紅燒羊肉
(Hung-shao-yang-jou)　Hangchow

Ingredients:
1 lb. (500 g) lamb
3 tablespoons oil
1 slice fresh ginger, crushed
½ teaspoon fennel seeds
1 tablespoon Chinese rice wine or sake
2 cups stock or water
6 tablespoons soy sauce
1 tablespoon sugar
1 clove garlic, crushed or minced

Method:
1. Blanch lamb in boiling water for 3 minutes and rinse thoroughly with cold water. Cut into 1-inch (3 cm) cubes.

2. Heat oil, add ginger and fennel seeds, cook and stir in oil for 1 minute. Add lamb, wine and stock, bring to a boil then simmer for 5 minutes.

3. Add soy sauce and sugar, cover, simmer for 2 hours. Stir in garlic and cook for 5 more minutes.

Egg & Chicken

Egg with Crab Meat

韭芽蟹腐皮
(*Chiu-ya-hsieh-fu-p'i*)   Shanghai

Ingredients:

½ cup crab meat, fresh, canned or frozen
5 eggs
1 lb. (500 g) Chinese chives or spinach
Mixture A:
    ½ teaspoon salt
    ½ tablespoon soy sauce
    1 tablespoon Chinese rice wine or sake
    dash of MSG (optional)
    dash of pepper
Mixture B:
    1 teaspoon salt
    1 teaspoon soy sauce
    1 teaspoon sesame oil
    pinch of sugar
    dash of MSG (optional)

Method:

1. Chop or flake the crab meat.
2. Beat eggs and mix in crab meat and mixture A.
3. Set a skillet over low heat, grease the bottom and the side of the pan. Gently pour in egg mixture, tip pan to cover the bottom of the pan entirely. When the mixture is almost dry, turn the whole thing over and cook the other side until dry. Transfer eggs to a cutting board and cut into 1½-inches (4 cm) by 1-inch (3 cm) pieces.
4. Wash chives, cut crosswise into 2-inch (6 cm) sections. Blanch and drain. When chives are cool mix in mixture B.
5. Arrange chives on a plate and place the eggs on top of them.

Note: In the original recipe, small fresh crabs (*hua-shao-p'ang-hsieh*) were used. When this kind of crab is available, first scrub and rinse under running water, then in a large mortar pound or crush with the pestle, wrap crabs in cheesecloth and squeeze out the crab juice. Mix the juice with eggs.

If the egg mixture does not set firm enough, add a small amount of cornstarch to the mixture before cooking.

Stir-fried Eggs
清炒雞蛋
(Ch'ing-ch'ao-chi-tan)　Peking

Ingredients:

3 eggs
pinch of salt
1 teaspoon minced scallions
½ cup chicken stock
1 tablespoon oil

Method:

1. Beat eggs, mix in salt, scallions and stock.
2. Heat oil, pour in eggs, stir and cook until eggs are thickened and slightly brown. Turn off heat when the eggs are beginning to thicken but still somewhat running.

Scrambled Egg with Tomatoes
鮮蕃茄炒蛋
(Hsien-fan-ch'ieh-ch'ao-tan)　Suchow

Ingredients:

½ lb. (250 g) tomatoes
3 eggs
1 teaspoon Chinese rice wine or sake
½ teaspoon salt
¼ cup chicken stock

Method:

1. Peel tomatoes and remove the seeds. Cut into ½-inch (1.5 cm) wedges.
2. Beat eggs and mix in wine and a pinch of salt.
3. Heat oil, stir-fry tomatoes for 1 minute, add ½ teaspoon salt and the beaten eggs. Stir and cook; when eggs begin to thicken, pour in chicken stock, stir constantly for 1 to 2 more minutes.

Whitebait Omelets
銀魚炒蛋
(Yin-yü-ch'ao-tan)　Suchow

Ingredients:

5 eggs
¼ lb. (125 g) whitebait
oil for deep-frying
Mixture A:
　1 teaspoon Chinese rice wine or sake
　½ egg white
　pinch of salt
　1 teaspoon cornstarch
Mixture B:
　1 teaspoon Chinese rice wine or sake
　1 teaspoon salt
　1 teaspoon cornstarch
　1 teaspoon scallions

Method:

1. Rinse whitebait and drain. Mix fish with mixture A.
2. Heat oil over high heat, deep-fry whitebait for 20 seconds and drain.
3. Beat eggs and mix in mixture B.
4. In a small skillet, heat 1 teaspoon oil until very hot, pour in about ¼ cup of egg mixture, when the eggs begin to set, add 1 tablespoon whitebait on top of eggs. Cook for 30 seconds or until eggs are completely thickened. Turn the pancake over and cook for another 30 seconds. Repeat the same procedure with the remaining egg mixture and fish.

Scallion Omelet

攤 雞 蛋

(T'an-chi-tan) Peking

Ingredients:

3 eggs
pinch of salt
1 tablespoon chopped scallions
½ tablespoon oil

Method:

1. Beat eggs, mix in salt and scallions.

2. In a skillet, heat oil over a moderate fire. Pour in egg mixture, tilt the pan to spread mixture evenly. Cook for 1 minute or until lightly browned. Turn the whole thing over and cook for another minute.

Pork Omelet

肉 絲 炒 蛋

(Jou-ssŭ-ch'ao-tan) Suchow

Ingredients:

4 eggs
¼ teaspoon salt
dash of MSG (optional)
2 oz. (50 g) lean pork
1 tablespoon oil
½ tablespoon Chinese rice wine or sake
1 teaspoon soy sauce
½ cup chicken stock

Method:

1. Beat eggs, mix in salt and MSG.

2. Cut pork into thin slivers, about 1½ inches (4 cm) long.

3. Heat oil, stir-fry pork until pinkish color is gone. Add eggs, wine, soy sauce and stock, stir and cook constantly for 2 minutes.

Egg with Bamboo Shoots

茭 白 炒 蛋

(Chiao-pai-ch'ao-tan) Shanghai

Ingredients:

¼ lb. (125 g) canned bamboo shoots
3 eggs
salt
dash of MSG (optional)
2 tablespoons oil
½ tablespoon lard or chicken fat
1 tablespoon minced scallions

Method:

1. Cut bamboo shoots into thin slivers, about 2 inches (6 cm) long.

2. Heat 1 tablespoon oil, stir-fry bamboo shoots with ⅛ teaspoon salt and a dash of MSG for 1 minute. Remove to plate.

3. Beat eggs, mix in a pinch of salt and a dash of MSG.

4. Heat the remaining tablespoon oil, pour in eggs, then add bamboo shoots, stir and cook until eggs begin to thicken. Add lard and mix thoroughly with eggs. Transfer to a serving plate and sprinkle scallions on top.

Note: Bamboo shoots are substituted for *chiao-pai*, a Chinese speciality.

Meat Omelets in Soup

烘 雞 蛋 餃
(*Hung-chi-tan-chiao*)　Chengtu

Ingredients:
1 tablespoon dried shrimp
2 oz. (50 g) bamboo shoots or water chestnuts, minced
1 cup spinach leaves
¼ lb. (125 g) ground pork
3 eggs
¼ teaspoon salt
oil
2 cups chicken stock
1 teaspoon lard or chicken fat
Mixture A:
   1 teaspoon minced scallions
   1 teaspoon cornstarch
   1 teaspoon soy sauce
   1 teaspoon oil

Method:
1. Soak dried shrimp in lukewarm water for 30 minutes and mince.

2. Wash spinach and discard tough leaves.

3. Mix pork with mixture A.

4. Beat eggs and add ⅛ teaspoon salt.

5. Heat 1 teaspoon oil in a metal ladle on top of the fire, swirl the oil around to grease the ladle evenly, empty oil. Add 2 to 3 tablespoons egg mixture into ladle and quickly swirl it about. When the eggs begin to thicken, but are not yet dry, place 1 tablespoon meat mixture in the center, then with a fork or a pair of chopsticks, fold one side of the omelet over the other side, forming a half-circle shaped miniature omelet. Repeat the same procedure with the remaining eggs and meat mixture.

6. In a saucepan, bring 2 cups stock to a boil, add spinach, ⅛ teaspoon salt and the omelets. Simmer over low heat 3 to 4 minutes or until the meat mixture is cooked.

Steamed Eggs

蒸蛋羹

(Chêng-tan-kêng) Peking

Ingredients:

3 eggs
1 tablespoon dried shrimp
2 tablespoons minced scallions
Mixture A:
   1 tablespoon soy sauce
   1 teaspoon salt
   1 tablespoon oil

Method:

1. Beat eggs, then mix in mixture A and 1¾ cups (350 cc) water or stock.

2. Rinse dried shrimp, cover with lukewarm water for 30 minutes and mince.

3. Pour the egg mixture into a bowl, then put the bowl in a steamer, cover and steam over low heat for 20 minutes.

4. When eggs are set, remove from steamer and sprinkle minced shrimp and scallions on top.

Note: For a richer taste, use chicken stock instead of water for the custard. When canned stock or bouillon cubes are used, cut down the amount of salt in mixture A. The soy sauce in mixture A can be poured over the steamed egg custard just before serving instead of mixing it with the eggs.

If there is foam floating on top of the egg mixture, break it apart with a spoon. Always steam eggs over a low fire to attain a smoother custard.

In Chinese cooking, steamed egg custard is considered a soup. Set the entire bowl on the dining table and with a tablespoon serve it in individual bowl.

(Variation 1)

Ingredients:

⅓ lb. (150 g) shrimp
2 oz. (50 g) cooked ham, minced
5 eggs, beaten
3 cups chicken stock
½ teaspoon salt
1 tablespoon chicken fat or oil

Method:

1. Shell shrimp and remove black vein. Rinse thoroughly, cut shrimp into pea-sized pieces.

2. Mix eggs with stock and salt. Steam over low heat for 10 minutes or until half set, drop in shrimp and chicken fat. Steam for 10 more minutes or until completely set.

(Variation 2)

Ingredients:

8–10 clams
1 tablespoon Chinese rice wine or sake
4 eggs, beaten
½ teaspoon salt

Method:

1. Soak clams in salted water for 1 hour, then boil them in 3 cups of water and 1 tablespoon wine. Remove clams from water as soon as they are open. Cool the clam stock and reserve.

2. Mix eggs with clam stock and salt. Place clams (shells and meat) in a large bowl, pour in egg mixture and steam for 20–30 minutes or until set.

Chicken with Spicy Sauce

怪 味 雞
(Kuai-wei-chi)　Chungking

Ingredients:
1 scallion, chopped
3 slices fresh ginger, crushed
1 whole chicken, about 3 lb. (1.5 kg)
10 Szechuan peppercorns
Mixture A:
　3 tablespoons soy sauce
　2 tablespoons vinegar
　1 tablespoon sesame oil
　1 teaspoon minced garlic
　1 teaspoon minced fresh ginger
　¼ teaspoon Szechuan peppercorn powder

Method:
1. Wash chicken thoroughly and place it in a large bowl.

2. Stuff the chicken cavity with ginger, scallion and Szechuan peppercorns. Place the bowl containing chicken in a steamer or in a large pan and steam for 30 minutes. Cool thoroughly.

3. In a small bowl, combine mixture A.

4. Remove bones from chicken and tear the meat into strips about ½ inch (1.5 cm) wide. Place chicken meat on a platter and pour mixture A over it.

Note: Cut-up chicken can be steamed in the same way as step 2. Decorate the platter with sliced cucumber as shown in the picture.

Braised Chicken

醬雞

(Chiang-chi) Suchow

Ingredients:

1 chicken, about 3 lb. (1.4 kg)
1 scallion, crushed
1 slice fresh ginger, about 1½ inches (4 cm) in
 diameter
Mixture A:
 1 tablespoon Chinese rice wine or sake
 5 tablespoons soy sauce
 2 tablespoons sugar
 ¼ teaspoon salt

Method:

1. Rinse chicken inside and out, then blanch in boiling water for 2 minutes.

2. Place chicken in a saucepan deep enough to hold the chicken, add ginger, scallion and mixture A. Fill the pan with water to cover the chicken. Bring to a boil and cook over a moderate flame for 30 minutes.

3. Remove chicken from sauce and let it cool for 15 minutes. With a cleaver, first cut off wings and legs, then split the chicken in half lengthwise. Chop each thigh and leg across the bones into 3 pieces; chop the breast and the back across the bones into pieces 1 inch (3 cm) wide. Arrange chicken with the skin side up on a platter and decorate with the wings and legs as shown in the picture.

Note: In this recipe chicken is substituted for duck.

Ducks are very popular on Chinese dining tables even in today's mainland China.

Braised Duck

醬鴨

(Chiang-ya) Suchow

Ingredients:

1 duck, 5 to 5½ lb. (2.5 kg)
1 leek, crushed and chopped
1½ tablespoons salt
3 slices fresh ginger, crushed
½ cup soy sauce
¼ lb. (125 g) sugar
3 tablespoons Chinese rice wine or sake
1 oz. (25 g) rice powder

Method:

1. Wash duck inside and out thoroughly. Rub duck with salt and put in a pot or a bowl. Place some heavy weight on top of the duck and refrigerate it for 48 hours.

2. Rinse duck thoroughly and blanch in 8 cups (1.5 liter) of boiling water for 2 minutes. Remove duck from water and rinse with cold water.

3. Remove scum from the boiling water, return the duck to the water, and add ginger, soy sauce, sugar, wine and rice powder. Cover and simmer for 30 minutes. Transfer duck to a plate and cool. Chop the duck up the same way as Braised Chicken.

Fried Chicken with Chestnuts

栗 子 雞

(Li-tzŭ-chi)   Shanghai

Ingredients:

1 lb. (500 g) chicken, unboned
2 scallions, cut into ½-inch (1.5 cm) sections
½ lb. (250 g) chestnuts
oil for deep-frying
1½ cups chicken stock
1 tablespoon cornstarch dissolved in 2 tablespoons water
½ teaspoon sesame oil
Mixture A:
   1 tablespoon Chinese rice wine or sake
   2 tablespoons soy sauce
   1 teaspoon sugar

Method:

1. Chop chicken across the bones into 1-inch
   (3 cm) pieces. Make a small cut through the
   skin of each chestnut. Cover chestnuts with
   water and boil for 1 minute, remove from
   heat. Peel off shell and inner skin.

2. In a small bowl, combine mixture A.

3. Heat oil and deep-fry chicken and chestnuts
   together for 30 seconds. Remove from oil and
   drain.

4. Empty all but 1 tablespoon oil from pan,
   stir-fry scallions for 30 seconds, add chicken,
   chestnuts, mixture A and chicken stock. Cover and cook for 3 minutes, thicken sauce with
   dissolved cornstarch and sprinkle with sesame
   oil.

Note: The chicken may be boned before cooking as
in the original recipe.

Braised Chicken with Potatoes

生 燒 塊 雞

(Shêng-shao-k'uai-chi)   Suchow

Ingredients:

¾ lb. (350 g) chicken unboned
½ lb. (250 g) potatoes
1 scallion, coarsely chopped
oil for deep-frying
1 tablespoon Chinese rice wine or sake
1 cup chicken stock
2 teaspoons cornstarch dissolved in 1 tablespoon
   water
few drops of sesame oil
Mixture A:
   2 tablespoons soy sauce
   1 tablespoon sugar
   ⅓ teaspoon salt

Method:

1. With a cleaver, chop chicken across the bones
   into 1½-inch (4 cm) pieces. Peel potatoes,
   then cut into 1-inch (3 cm) wedges.

2. Heat oil over moderate heat until hot, drop in
   chicken and fry for one minute. Empty all
   the oil leaving chicken in the pan. Pour wine
   over the chicken and stir in scallion, mixture
   A, potatoes and stock. Cover and simmer
   over medium heat until potatoes are tender.

3. Thicken sauce with dissolved cornstarch and
   sprinkle with sesame oil.

Note: Potatoes may be deep-fried before adding
to the chicken. In the original recipe, yams were used
instead of potatoes. For variations, substitute taro
roots for potatoes.

Fried Chicken with Bamboo Shoots

炸 溜 小 雞

(Cha-liu-hsiao-chi) Tsingtao

Ingredients:

1 lb. (500 g) chicken with bones
2 tablespoons soy sauce
1 tablespoon cornstarch
1 teaspoon cloud ears
⅓ lb. (125 g) canned bamboo shoots
1 clove garlic, minced
1 teaspoon minced fresh ginger
1 scallion, chopped
oil for deep-frying
1½ tablespoons vinegar
½ cup chicken stock
dash of MSG (optional)
1 tablespoon cornstarch dissolved in 2 tablespoons water
few drops sesame oil

Method:

1. With a cleaver, chop chicken across the bones into 1-inch (3 cm) pieces. In a bowl, mix chicken with soy sauce and 1 tablespoon cornstarch.

2. Soak cloud ears in hot water for 30 minutes. Rinse thoroughly and remove the woody parts of the stems. Cut bamboo shoots into very thin slices about 1½ inches (4 cm) long and ½ inch (1.5 cm) wide.

3. Heat oil over medium heat to 350°F., deep-fry chicken until golden brown. With a strainer, remove chicken all at once from oil.

4. Empty all but 3 tablespoons oil from pan, stir-fry garlic, ginger and scallion for 20 seconds. Add cloud ears, vinegar and stock,

bring to a rapid boil. Skim off scum, if any.

5. Add MSG, thicken sauce with dissolved cornstarch, then stir in fried chicken and cook 30 more seconds.

Steamed Chicken in a Bowl

元 盅 雞

(Yuan-chung-chi) Suchow

Ingredients:

¾ lb. (350 g) chicken
2 oz. (50 g) cooked Smithfield ham
1 slice fresh ginger, about 1½ inches (4 cm) in diameter
¼ lb. (125 g) canned bamboo shoots
1 scallion, chopped
1 tablespoon Chinese rice wine or sake
1 teaspoon salt
a few trefoil leaves or spinach leaves

Method:

1. Chop chicken across the bones into 1-inch (3 cm) pieces.

2. Cut ham and fresh ginger into thin slivers. Chop bamboo shoots coarsely.

3. In a saucepan, blanch chicken in 5 cups of boiling water, remove chicken from water and place in a deep bowl with the skin side up. Add wine and salt to the chicken water and bring to a boil.

4. Add ham, bamboo shoots, scallion and ginger to the chicken. Pour chicken stock into the bowl containing chicken, then place a piece of paper over the bowl and steam for 2 hours. Add the trefoil leaves to soup before serving.

Fish & Shellfish

Deep-fried Fish with Vegetables
干燒加吉魚
(Kan-shao-chia-chi-yü) Tsingtao

Ingredients:
1 fish, 1½ lb. (500g – 600g), sea bream or red snapper
3 dried Chinese mushrooms
1 chili pepper, cut into thin slivers
2 oz. (50 g) pork, cut into thin slivers
1 oz. (25 g) canned bamboo shoots, slivered
1 oz. (25 g) Szechuan preserved vegetable (*cha-ts'ai*, page 8), slivered
1 scallion, slivered
½ tablespoon slivered fresh ginger
1 tablespoon soy sauce
oil for deed-frying
Mixture A:
  2 tablespoons soy sauce
  2 tablespoons sugar
  1 tablespoon Chinese rice wine or sake
  2 teaspoons sweet bean paste (*t'ien-mien-chiang*, page 14)
  1 teaspoon brown bean paste (*tou-pan-chiang*, page 11)

½ teaspoon salt
2½ cups chicken stock

Method:
1. Soak mushrooms in water for 20 minutes, cut into thin slivers.

2. Scale and clean fish, then score both sides of fish by making 3–4 diagonal cuts about ½ inch (1.5 cm) deep and 1 inch (3 cm) apart.

3. Dry fish thoroughly with paper towels and coat with 1 tablespoon soy sauce. Deep-fry fish in very hot oil until golden brown. Baste continually with the hot oil.

4. In a pan, heat 3 tablespoons oil over a medium flame, add mushrooms, pork, bamboo shoots, Szechuan preserved vegetable, scallion and ginger, stir-fry all the ingredients for 1 minute. Add fish and mixture A, simmer 15 minutes or until the sauce has been reduced by half. Transfer fish to a serving plate, pour vegetables and sauce over it.

Sweet-and-Sour Carp
糖醋鯉魚
(T'ang-ts'u-li-yü) Peking

Ingredients:

1 carp, 1½ lb. (750 g)
2 tablespoons cornstarch
oil for deep-frying
2 tablespoons oil
1 tablespoon cornstarch dissolved in 2 tablespoons water
Mixture A:
   3 tablespoons vinegar
   5 tablespoons sugar
   1 tablespoon soy sauce
   1 tablespoon Chinese rice wine or sake
   1 teaspoon salt
   ¼ cup chicken stock

Method:

1. Scale and clean fish, score both sides of fish
   by making 3–4 diagonal cuts about ½ inch
   (1.5 cm) deep and 1 inch (3 cm) apart.

2. Dry fish thoroughly with paper towels, then
   coat inside and out with a paste made of 3
   tablespoons of cornstarch and equal amount
   of water.

3. Heat oil, lower fish into oil and deep-fry for
   15 minutes over a moderate fire. With a ladle,
   baste fish continually with hot oil. When fish
   becomes crisp and golden brown, remove
   from oil and drain. Place fish on a serving
   platter.

4. Heat the remaining oil, add mixture A, bring
   to a boil and thicken sauce with dissolved
   cornstarch. Pour sauce over fish and serve.

Fried Carp with Vegetables
紅燒鯉魚
(Hung-Shao-li-yü) Peking

Ingredients:

1 carp, 1 lb. (500 g)
2 oz. (50 g) pork, cut into thin slices
1 oz. (30 g) canned bamboo shoots, cut in thin
   slices
1 scallion, cut into 1½-inch (4.5 cm) sections
oil for deep-frying
Mixture A:
   2 tablespoons Chinese rice wine or sake
   3 tablespoons soy sauce
   3 tablespoons sugar
   2 teaspoons vinegar
   dash of MSG (optional)
   2½ cups chicken stock

Method:

1. Scale and clean fish, score both sides of fish
   by making 7 diagonal cuts about ½ inch (1.5
   cm) deep.

2. Heat oil and deep-fry fish 10 minutes or until
   crisp. Place fish on a serving plate.

3. In a wok or skillet, heat 1 tablespoon oil and
   stir-fry scallion, ginger and bamboo shoots
   for 30 seconds. Add mixture A and bring to
   a boil, then thicken sauce with dissolved
   cornstarch. Pour sauce over fish and serve.

Steamed Fish

清蒸鯽魚

(Ch'ing-chêng-chi-yü)　Suchow

Ingredients:

2 gold carp, about ⅔ lb. (300 g) each
2 tablespoons Chinese rice wine or sake
4 dried Chinese mushrooms
¼ cup sliced bamboo shoots, about ⅔ inch
　(2 cm) wide
¼ cup sliced Smithfield ham, about ⅓ inch
　(1 cm) wide
pinch of salt
½ tablespoon slivered fresh ginger
1 tablespoon coarsely chopped scallions
2–3 tablespoons chicken stock
1 teaspoon lard or oil

Method:

1. Soak mushrooms in water for 30 minutes then
cut into slivers.

2. Scale and clean fish, score both sides of each
fish by making 3 diagonal cuts about ¼ inch
(1 cm) deep. Rub fish with wine.

3. Place fish on a platter, sprinkle with salt and
scallion on top of fish, then pour stock over
them.

4. Steam fish for 15 minutes over high heat.
Remove and discard ginger and scallions.
Fresh scallion strips may be garnished for
decoration.

Note: The fish in the picture is substituted for gold
carp. Sea bass, perch, sea trout or striped bass may
be cooked in the same way.

Fried Fish Fillets

焦炒魚条

(Chiao-ch'ao-yü-t'iao)　Tsingtao

Ingredients:

½ lb. (250 g) white meat fish fillets
1 scallion, cut into 2-inch (6 cm) sections
1 clove garlic, sliced
1 slice fresh ginger, slivered
oil for deep-frying
flour for dusting
few drops sesame oil
Mixture A:
　1½ tablespoons soy sauce
　¼ cup chicken stock
　½ tablespoon Chinese rice wine or sake
　½ tablespoon vinegar
　1 teaspoon sugar
　dash of MSG

Method:

1. Cut fish fillets into 1-inch (3 cm) by 2-inch
(6 cm) rectangles about ½ inch (1.5 cm)
thick. Dust with flour.

2. Heat oil and deep-fry fish until crisp and
slightly browned.

3. Heat the remaining oil, stir-fry scallion, garlic
and ginger for 30 seconds, add fish, mixture A
and sesame oil.

Note: Fresh water fish was used in the original recipe, but any firm white fish fillets, either fresh water
or salt water variety, may be used.

Fish and
Bean Curd Soup

草魚豆腐

(Ts'ao-yü-tou-fu) Shanghai

Ingredients:

1 square bean curd, about 3″ × 3″ (7.5 × 7.5 cm)

⅓ lb. (150 g) white meat fish fillets

1 oz. (20 g) pickled mustard greens (red-in-snow, page 9)

1 scallion, cut into 2-inch (6 cm) sections

2 tablespoons oil

2½ cups chicken stock

1 teaspoon lard or oil

Mixture A:

    1 tablespoon Chinese rice wine or sake

    1 tablespoon sugar

    2 tablespoons soy sauce

Method:

1. Soak pickled mustard greens for 15 minutes and chop.

2. Cut bean curd into 1½-inch (4 cm) squares about ½-inch (1.5 cm) thick. Cut fish fillets into same size.

3. Heat oil until it begins to smoke, stir-fry fish and pickled mustard greens for 30 seconds, add mixture A and stock. Bring to a boil, put in bean curd and turn the heat down, simmer soup for 6 minutes. When bean curd floats to the top, add lard and scallion.

Clear Fish Soup

川魚片

(Ch'uan-yü-p'ien) Hangchow

Ingredients:

½ lb. (250 g) white meat fish fillets

2 cups chicken stock

1 teaspoon Chinese rice wine or sake

pinch of salt

¼ lb. (125 g) canned bamboo shoots, sliced

dash of MSG (optional)

1 cup trefoil or spinach

1 teaspoon lard or oil

Method:

1. Cut fish fillets into 1-inch (3 cm) by 2-inch (6 cm) rectangles and about ½ inch (1.5 cm) thick. Mix fish with wine and salt. Let stand for 10 minutes.

2. Bring stock to a boil, add fish. Simmer gently for 1 minute. With a slotted spoon, transfer fish to a large soup bowl.

3. Skim off scum from soup, add bamboo shoots and bring to a boil. Drop in vegetables and season with pinch of salt and MSG.

4. Heat soup thoroughly then pour into soup bowl containing fish, add lard and serve.

Stir-fried Fish with Vegetables

鮮魚丁

(Hsien-yü-ting) Shantung

Ingredients:

⅔ lb. (350 g) white meat fish fillets
1 tablespoon cornstarch
1 egg white
oil for deep-frying
¼ lb. (125 g) canned bamboo shoots, diced
1 scallion, cut into 1-inch (3 cm) sections
1 clove garlic, sliced
¼ cup defrosted frozen peas
Mixture A:
   ½ cup chicken stock
   1 tablespoon soy sauce
   2 teaspoons cornstarch
   pinch of salt
   1 teaspoon Chinese rice wine or sake
   dash of MSG (optional)

Method:

1. Dice fish fillets, and mix with 1 tablespoon cornstarch and 1 egg white.

2. Heat oil, and deep-fry fish cubes, stir continually to separate fish. With a strainer remove fish from oil and drain.

3. Combine mixture A and green peas.

4. Heat 2 tablespoons oil, stir-fry scallion and garlic for 30 seconds, add mixture A and bamboo shoots. Stir a few times then add fish, blend thoroughly and serve.

Fillet of Fish with Wine Sauce

糟露魚片

(Tsao-lu-yü-p'ien) Suchow

Ingredients:

⅔ lb. (350 g) white meat fish fillets
1 tablespoon Chinese rice wine or sake
¼ teaspoon salt
1 egg white
1 tablespoon cornstarch
oil for deep-frying
2 tablespoons oil
1 tablespoon minced scallions
Mixture A:
   1 clove garlic, minced
   1 oz. (20 g) wine lees (wine rice) or 3 tablespoons sake
   ¼ cup chicken stock

Method:

1. Cut fish fillets into 2-inch (6 cm) by ⅔-inch (2 cm) rectangles. Mix fish with wine, salt, cornstarch and egg white.

2. In a small bowl combine mixture A.

3. Heat oil and deep-fry fish for 1 minute, with a strainer, remove fish and drain. Set aside.

4. Heat the remaining 2 tablespoons oil, stir-fry scallions for 15 seconds, add mixture A and bring to a boil. Add fish and blend thoroughly with the sauce. Sprinkle with sesame oil and serve.

Sweet-and-Sour Fish Fillets

荔枝魚塊
(Li-chih-yü-k'uai)   Hangchow

Ingredients:
½ lb. (250 g) fish fillets
1 small cucumber
½ onion
3 tablespoons cornstarch
3 tablespoons flour
3 tablespoons oil
oil for deep-frying
few drops of sesame oil
Mixture A:
    3 tablespoons soy sauce
    3 tablespoons vinegar
    3 tablespoons sugar

Method:
1. Cut fish fillets into 1⅓-inch (3.5 cm) squares and about ½ inch (1.5 cm) thick.

2. Cut cucumber into wedges approximately the same size as the fish fillet squares. Cut onion lengthwise into 3–4 sections then separate each layer.

3. Mix cornstarch and flour with some water to make a thick batter.

4. Heat oil, coat fish squares with batter and deep-fry over high heat until slightly browned.

5. Heat remaining oil, add cucumber and onion, stir-fry for 1 minute. Add fish and mixture A, cook and blend thoroughly. When sauce is thickened, sprinkle a few drops of sesame oil on top and serve.

Fried Fish with Vinegar Sauce

醋 魚

(Ts'u-yü) Suchow

Ingredients:

⅔ lb. (350 g) white meat fish fillets
1 scallion, coarsely chopped
½ teaspoon fresh ginger juice, or 1 teaspoon
   minced ginger
2 tablespoons oil
1 tablespoon Chinese rice wine or sake
1½ cups chicken stock
1½ tablespoons vinegar
1½ tablespoons sugar
1 tablespoon cornstarch dissolved in 2 tablespoons water
1 teaspoon sesame oil
Mixture A:
   3 tablespoons soy sauce
   1½ tablespoons sugar
   1 tablespoon vinegar

Method:

1. Cut fish fillets into 2-inch (6 cm) by ½-inch
   (1.5 cm) strips about ½ inch (1.5 cm) thick.

2. Heat oil, stir-fry scallion until browned. Add
   fish and wine, turn fish gently and cook for
   1 minute. Pour in mixture A, stock and ginger
   juice. Simmer 5 minutes.

3. Add vinegar and sugar then thicken sauce
   with dissolved cornstarch and sprinkle with
   sesame oil.

Fried Fish in Soup

爆 川

(Pao-ch'uan) Suchow

Ingredients:

½ lb. (250 g) white meat fish fillets
2 tablespoons oil
oil for deep-frying
1 scallion, cut into 2-inch (6 cm) sections
2 teaspoons Chinese rice wine or sake
2 teaspooons sugar
1 cup chicken stock
pinch of salt
2 oz. (100 g) mung bean noodles, soaked
1 teaspoon sesame oil
Mixture A:
   1 tablespoon soy sauce
   ½ tablespoon Chinese rice wine or sake
   ½ teaspoon ginger juice, or 1 teaspoon minced
      ginger
   ½ stalk scallion, cut into 2-inch (6 cm) sections

Method:

1. Cut fish fillets into 2-inch (6 cm) by 1-inch
   (3 cm) strips, about ½-inch (1.5 cm) thick.
   Marinate fish with mixture A for 1 hour.
   Drain and pat dry with paper towels.

2. Heat oil over medium fire, deep-fry fish for
   1 minute, then turn heat up to high and fry
   until fish strips are crisp and golden brown.

3. Heat the remaining oil, stir-fry scallion for
   20 seconds, add fish, ginger juice, sugar and
   1½ cups water. Bring everything to a rapid
   boil, reduce heat and simmer for 5 minutes.

4. Turn heat to high, add stock, soy sauce, salt
   and mung bean noodles, boil for 1 minute
   then add sesame oil and serve.

bowl. To the saucepan add lard, MSG, chives, mushrooms and ham. Bring the stock to a boil and pour into the bowl and serve.

very good

Fried Fish with Brown Bean Sauce

豆瓣鮮魚

(Tou-pan-hsien-yü)   Chungking

Ingredients:
1 lb. (500 g) white meat fish fillets
2 chili peppers, seeded and minced
1 clove garlic, minced
1 teaspoon minced fresh ginger
1 tablespoon minced scallions
oil for deep-frying
⅓ cup hot water
1 tablespoon vinegar
½ tablespoon cornstarch dissolved in 1 tablespoon water
Mixture A:
   1 tablespoon brown bean sauce *(tou-pan-chiang*, page 11)
   3 tablespoons soy sauce
   1½ tablespoons sugar

Method:
1. Cut fish fillets into 2-inch (6 cm) squares.

2. Heat oil, and deep-fry fish for 2 minutes. Remove from oil and drain.

3. Empty all but 2 tablespoons oil from pan, stir-fry chili peppers, garlic and ginger for 30 seconds, add mixture A. Add fish and simmer 3 minutes or until most of the liquid has been evaporated.

4. Add 1 tablespoon vinegar to fish and thicken sauce with dissolved cornstarch. Transfer fish to a serving plate and garnish with minced scallions.

Fish Ball Soup

清湯魚圓

Bland
Needs re-seasoning

(Ch'ing-t'ang-yü-yuan)   Hangchow

Ingredients:
1 teaspoon minced fresh ginger *less*
1 tablespoon chopped Chinese chives
3 dried mushrooms
3 slices cooked Smithfield ham
⅔ lb. (300 g) white meat fish fillets
½ teaspoon salt
1 teaspoon lard or oil
dash of MSG (optional)
4–5 cups chicken stock

[1–2 scallions, cut in 1" lengths – into soup]

Method:
1. Soak mushrooms in lukewarm water for 20 minutes and cut into strips about ½ inch (1.5 cm) wide. In a small saucepan boil mushrooms for 10 minutes. Cut ham into strips 1½ inches (4 cm) long and ⅔ inch (2 cm) wide.

2. Dice fish, chop and pound the fish with the blunt side of a cleaver until it becomes a paste; or use a meat grinder and grind the fish 2–3 times. *Use processor steel blade.* [During chopping, add a little at a time, about 3 tablespoons water] and ½ teaspoon salt. *Chop ginger + chives into fish paste.* In a bowl, beat fish paste vigorously; as you beat, add gradually 3 tablespoons water, beat until mixture becomes rubbery. To form the fish mixture into small balls about 1 inch (3 cm) in diameter, ~~take a handful of fish mixture, and forming the hand into a fist, gently squeeze a teaspoonful of fish paste up between the index finger and thumb,~~ *use* ~~then~~ scoop up the ball with a teaspoon. Drop the fish balls into a saucepan containing cold water. *Put in wet plate + refrigerate till ready to use.*

3. Set the saucepan containing fish balls over a moderate flame and heat slowly until the fish balls are cooked, about 8 to 10 minutes. With a slotted spoon transfer fish balls to a serving

100

Fish and Bean Curd Soup

酸辣黃魚豆腐
(*Suan-la-huang-yü-tou-fu*)　Shanghai

Ingredients:
1 fish, ½ lb. (250 g), sea bass or sea trout
1 tablespoon soy sauce
½ teaspoon minced fresh ginger
1 tablespoon chopped trefoil or spinach or fresh
   coriander
1 scallion, cut into ½-inch (1.5 cm) sections
1 tablespoon chopped scallions
1 square bean curd, about 3″ × 3″ (7.5 × 7.5
   cm)
3 tablespoons oil
2 cups chicken stock or water
dash of pepper
2 tablespoons vinegar
Mixture A:
   2 tablespoons soy sauce
   1 tablespoon Chinese rice wine or sake
   2 teaspoons sugar
   pinch of salt
   dash of MSG (optional)

Method:
1. Scale and clean fish. Cut crosswise into two
   sections. Rub fish with 1 tablespoon soy
   sauce.
2. Heat 2 tablespoons oil, place fish in pan and
   brown for 3 minutes on each side. Remove to
   plate.
3. Heat the remaining oil, stir-fry ginger and
   scallion sections for 20 seconds, return fish
   to pan, add mixture A and 1½ cups stock or
   water. Bring to a boil, then simmer over low
   heat for 10 minutes. Add bean curd and ½
   cup water, cook 3 more minutes.
4. In a soup bowl, put in pepper, vinegar, trefoil
   and chopped scallions, then pour the fish soup
   into the bowl and serve.

Braised Fish in Soy Sauce

紅燒頭尾
(*Hung-shao-t'ou-wei*)　Hangchow

Ingredients:
1 fish, ⅔ lb. (300 g), sea bream or flounder
½ tablespoon soy sauce
1 tablespoon dried cloud ears
1 scallion, slivered
2 oz. (50 g) canned bamboo shoots, sliced
½ tablespoon slivered fresh ginger
3 tablespoons oil
1 teaspoon cornstarch dissolved in 1 tablespoon
   water
½ teaspoon sesame oil
Mixture A:
   4 tablespoons soy sauce
   1 tablespoon Chinese rice wine or sake
   1 tablespoon sugar
   ½–1 cup chicken stock
   dash of MSG (optional)

Method:
1. Soak cloud ears in hot water for 30 minutes
   and rinse.
2. Scale and clean fish. Cut crosswise into two
   sections. Rub fish with ½ tablespoon soy
   sauce.
3. Heat oil until it begins to smoke, place fish
   in pan and brown for 3 minutes on each side.
   Add mixture A, cloud ears, scallion, bamboo
   shoots and ginger, cover and simmer 10 minutes.
4. Thicken sauce with dissolved cornstarch and
   add sesame oil.

Note: In the original recipe, only the head and tail
of a large fish were used for this dish.

Steamed Scabbard Fish

煎 蒸 带 魚
(Chien-chêng-tai-yü) Peking

Ingredients:

1 lb. (500 g) scabbard fish
1 teaspoon salt
½ scallion, slivered
1 slice fresh ginger, slivered
½ tablespoon chopped fresh coriander or trefoil
2–3 tablespoons oil
few drops of sesame oil
Mixture A:
    2 cups chicken stock
    1 teaspoon salt

Method:

1. Clean fish, cut crosswise into 2-inch (6 cm) sections. Score each side crosswise with 2 cuts about 1 inch (3 cm) wide and ¼ inch (1 cm) deep. Sprinkle with salt.

2. Heat oil, brown both sides of fish.

3. Place fish in a heat proof plate, add mixture A, arrange ginger and scallion on top of fish and steam for 20 to 30 minutes. Uncover pan, add coriander and sprinkle sesame oil on top.

Note: For a variation, skip step 3, simply brown until cooked and serve fish with soy sauce mixed with sesame oil as dip.

Fried Scabbard Fish with Sesame Sauce
香肥带魚
(Hsiang-fei-tai-yü) Shanghai

Ingredients:
2/3 lb. (300 g) scabbard fish
1 tablespoon Chinese rice wine or sake
pinch of salt
dash of pepper
1/2 teaspoon sesame oil
oil for deep-frying
cornstarch for dusting
1/2 cup milk
1 tablespoon tomato ketchup
2/3 teaspoon salt
1/2 tablespoon cornstarch dissolved in 1 tablespoon water
1/2 teaspoon toasted sesame seeds

Method:
1. Clean fish, cut crosswise into 1 2/3-inch (5 cm) sections, then cut the pieces lengthwise into pieces 1/2 inch (1.5 cm) wide.

2. In a bowl, mix fish with wine, salt, pepper and sesame oil.

3. Heat oil, dredge fish with cornstarch and deep-fry until slightly browned. Drain and place fish on a plate.

4. Empty all but 1 tablespoon oil from pan, add 1/3 cup water, bring to a boil. Then add milk, ketchup, the remaining 2/3 teaspoon salt. When sauce comes to a rapid boil, thicken with dissolved cornstarch. Pour sauce over fish and sprinkle with sesame seeds.

Stir-fried Cuttlefish with Scallion
爆炒墨魚花
(Pao-ch'ao-mo-yü-hua) Tsingtao

Ingredients:
1/2 lb. (250 g) cuttlefish
1 clove garlic, sliced
1 scallion, cut into 1-inch (3 cm) sections
oil for deep-frying
2–3 tablespoons oil
1 teaspoon lard or oil
Mixture A:
   1/2 teaspoon salt
   1/2 cup chicken stock
   2 teaspoons Chinese rice wine or sake
   2 teaspoons cornstarch

Method:
1. Remove skin from cuttlefish. Score the surface with crisscross cuts, then cut into 1/2-inch (1.5 cm) squares.

2. Blanch cuttlefish for 30 seconds and drain.

3. Heat oil and deep-fry cuttlefish for 1 minute, and drain.

4. In a small bowl, combine mixture A.

5. Heat remaining oil, stir-fry garlic and scallion for 15 seconds. Add cuttlefish, mixture A and lard, blend thoroughly and serve.

Note: Cuttlefish is called *mo-yü* or *wu-tse-yü* in Chinese. The name for this dish, *mo-yü-hua*, means "cuttlefish blossoms," because of the way it is cut resembles a flower.

Fried Prawns with Spinach Batter

翡翠蝦仁
(*Fei-t'sui-hsia-jen*)   Tientsin

Ingredients:

1 lb. (500 g) medium-sized shrimp
2 oz. (50 g) ham, diced
2 oz. (50 g) canned bamboo shoots, diced
¼ lb. (125 g) spinach
pinch of salt
2–3 tablespoons cornstarch
oil for deep-frying
1 tablespoon minced scallions
Mixture A:
   1 tablespoon Chinese rice wine or sake
   ½ tablespoon sugar
   1 teaspoon ginger juice
   pinch of salt
   dash of MSG (optional)

Method:

1. Shell and devein shrimp. Rinse thoroughly and drain.

2. Wash spinach and boil for 1 minute, drain. Purée spinach in a blender or by chopping. Wrap spinach paste with cheesecloth, squeeze by hand and extract the green juice into a bowl. Mix spinach juice and cornstarch to form a thick batter.

3. Coat shrimp with spinach batter.

4. Heat oil and deep-fry shrimp over a low fire. Stir occasionally to separate shrimp. As soon as shrimp come to surface, remove and drain.

5. Empty all but 2 to 3 tablespoons oil from pan, stir-fry scallions for 10 seconds, add ham, bamboo shoots, shrimp and mixture A. Stir and cook for 1 more minute.

Note: *Fei-t'sui* means emerald, since the shrimp are coated with green batter, hence it looks like jade.

Shrimp with Tomato Sauce

蕃茄蝦仁
(Fan-ch'ieh-hsia-jen) Tsingtao

Ingredients:
½ lb. (250 g) shelled shrimp
½ egg
pinch of salt
1–2 tablespoons cornstarch
oil for deep-frying
⅔ lb. (300 g) tomatoes
2–3 tablespoons oil
¼ cup defrosted frozen peas
2 teaspoons cornstarch dissolved in 1 tablespoon
　　water
few drops sesame oil
Mixture A:
　　2½ teaspoons sugar
　　¼ teaspoon salt
　　½ Chinese rice wine or sake
　　⅓ chicken stock
　　dash of MSG (optional)

Method:
1. Remove black veins from shrimp. Wash and drain.
2. Mix together egg, salt and cornstarch. Dip shrimp in batter and deep-fry for one minute. Stir to separate shrimp. Drain well.
3. Blanch tomatoes and peel. Cut crosswise and remove seeds, then cut tomatoes into ⅔-inch (2 cm) square.
4. Heat oil, stir-fry peas and tomatoes for 1 minute. Add mixture A and thicken sauce with dissolved cornstarch. Stir in shrimp then sprinkle sesame oil for flavor.

Note: When fresh tomatoes are not available, add 3 tablespoons tomato ketchup to mixture A and reduce the amount of sugar. To enrich the color more green peas have been added in this recipe than in the original one.

Plain Stir-fried Shrimp

清蝦仁
(Ch'ing-hsia-jen) Suchow

Ingredients:
⅔ lb. (300 g) shelled shrimp
⅔ teaspoon salt
1 egg white
2–3 teaspoons cornstarch
oil for deep-frying
1 tablespoon Chinese rice wine or sake
2–3 tablespoons chicken stock
1 teaspoon cornstarch dissolved in 1 tablespoon
　　water
few drops sesame oil

Method:
1. Remove black veins from shrimp, wash and drain. Marinate shrimp with salt, cornstarch and egg white.
2. Heat oil and deep-fry shrimp for 1 minute. Stir and separate shrimp. With a strainer, remove shrimp from oil and drain.
3. Empty all but 2 to 3 tablespoons oil from pan, add wine, stock and shrimp. Thicken sauce with dissolved cornstarch and sprinkle with sesame oil.

Note: For a more decorative look, surround shrimp with green vegetables on plate.
　　In the original recipe, the shrimp was marinated for 1 to 2 hours in egg and cornstarch mixture before cooking. But if you mix shrimp thoroughly by hand, it is unnecessary to wait.
　　Be sure not to overcook shrimp.

Braised Shrimp

干燒大蝦
(*Kan-shao-ta-hsia*)   Tsingtao

Ingredients:
1 lb. (500 g) jumbo shrimp
1 slice fresh ginger, minced
1 tablespoon minced scallions
oil for deep-frying
Mixture A:
    1½ tablespoons Chinese rice wine or sake
    2 tablespoons soy sauce
    2 tablespoons sugar
    ½ cup chicken stock

Method:
1. Trim off legs and tail tips of shrimp. Rinse thoroughly, squeeze water from tail tips. With a knife make an incision on the back of each shrimp and remove black veins. Cut each one crosswise in two, and pat dry with paper towels.

2. Heat oil over a high flame, deep-fry shrimp for 2 minutes or until they turn bright red. Remove from oil and drain.

3. Empty all but 2 tablespoons oil from pan, stir-fry ginger and scallions for 15 seconds, add mixture A and shrimp. Stir thoroughly, transfer to plate and serve.

Note: This shrimp dish is very popular. The seasonings may vary depending on the region. In Szechuan, the sauce is seasoned with chili peppers and brown bean paste.
    Follow this basic recipe and create your own version of sauce by reducing the sugar and adding ketchup to enhance the taste and give color contrast.

Stir-fried Shrimp Patties

炒 蝦 餅
(Ch'ao-hsia-ping)　Suchow

Ingredients:
⅔ lb. (300 g) shelled shrimp
¼ lb. (100 g) pork fat, minced
2 oz. (tp g) canned bamboo shoots, minced
1 tablespoon minced scallions
1 egg white
3–4 tablespoons oil
10 oz. (300 g) spinach
pinch of salt
¼ cup chicken stock
½ tablespoon Chinese rice wine or sake
1 teaspoon cornstarch dissolved in 1 tablespoon
　water
few drops sesame oil
Mixture A:
　1 teaspoon cornstarch
　½ tablespoon Chinese rice wine or sake
　⅔ teaspoon salt

Method:
1. Remove black veins from shrimp, rinse and drain. Chop or grind shrimp into a paste, place shrimp paste in a bowl, mix in pork fat, bamboo shoots, scallions, mixture A and egg white. Form mixture into patties 1½ inches (5 cm) in diameter.

2. Heat oil in a skillet and brown patties on both sides, set aside.

3. Stir-fry spinach in 1 tablespoon oil, pinch of salt and ¼ cup water, cover and cook 1 minute or until tender. Drain off juice and arrange into an even layer on a plate.

4. Bring stock and wine to a boil, then thicken with dissolved corsntarch, blend in shrimp patties and add sesame oil. Place patties on top of spinach and serve.

Shrimp with Bean Curd Soup
三蝦豆腐
(San-hsia-tou-fu) Shanghai

Ingredients:
¼ lb. (100 g) shelled shrimp
¼ lb. (100 g) canned bamboo shoots, diced
2 oz. (50 g) lean pork, diced
1 square bean curd, 3″ × 3″ (7.5 × 7.5 cm), diced
2½ tablespoons shrimp sauce
3 cups chicken stock
½ teaspoon salt
1⅓ tablespoons cornstarch dissolved in 3 tablespoons water
1 teaspoon lard (optional)

Method:
1. Remove black veins from shrimp, rinse and drain.
2. In a bowl, mix shrimp, bamboo shoots, pork and shrimp sauce by hand.
3. Bring to a boil stock, shrimp, bamboo shoots, pork and bean curd. Season with salt and MSG thicken with dissolved cornstarch, then add lard, if desired.

Boiled Shrimp
鹽水蝦
(Yen-shui-hsia) Suchow

Ingredients:
1 lb. (500 g) medium-sized shrimp
2 sections scallion, 2 inch (6 cm) long, crushed
1 sliced fresh ginger, slightly crushed
Mixture A:
  1 tablespoon Chinese rice wine or sake
  2 tablespoons salt

Method:
1. Wash shrimp thoroughly and drain.
2. Boil ginger and scallion in 3 cups water for 2 minutes. Add shrimp and mixture A, boil until shrimp become red. Skim off scum, if any. With a strainer, remove shrimp from stock.
3. Set stock away from heat and cool. Remove and discard scallion and ginger. Return shrimp to stock and soak for 30 to 60 minutes. Drain and arrange shrimp on plate.

Note: Large live shrimp were used in the original recipe.

Stir-fried Shrimp with Pork Kidney

炒 蝦 腰

(Ch'ao-hsia-yao)   Suchow

Ingredients:

1 pork kidney
3 dried mushrooms, soaked, stemmed and cut
   each one in half
2 oz. (50 g) canned bamboo shoots, sliced
1 scallion, cut into 1½-inch (4 cm) sections
2 oz. (50 g) shelled shrimp
¼ egg white (optional)
pinch of salt
2 teaspoons cornstarch
oil for deep-frying
1 tablespoon cornstarch dissolved in 1 tablespoon water
few drops sesame oil

Method:

1. Cut kidney lengthwise in half and remove any
   white membrane. Rinse thoroughly in several
   changes of water. Score the surface and make
   a crisscross pattern then cut into 1½-inch
   (4.5 cm) by 1-inch (3 cm) pieces. Blanch kidney in boiling water for 1 minute and drain.

2. Remove black veins from shrimp, wash and
   drain. Mix with egg white, salt and cornstarch. Deep-fry shrimp and kidney separately
   each for 1 minute.

3. Stir-fry mushrooms and bamboo shoots in 3
   tablespoons oil for 2 minutes, add mixture A.
   Thicken sauce with dissolved cornstarch, then
   blend in shrimp and kidney, sprinkle with
   sesame oil and serve.

Crab Meat with Bean Curd

蟹 粉 豆 腐

(Hsieh-fên-tou-fu)   Suchow

Ingredients:

2 oz. (50 g) frozen or canned crab meat
2 squares bean curd, 3″ × 3″ (7.5 × 7.5 cm) each
3 tablespoons oil
1 tablespoon minced scallions
¾ cup chicken stock
½ tablespoon cornstarch, dissolved in
   1 tablespoon water
1 teaspoon minced fresh ginger
Mixture A:
   1½ tablespoons soy sauce
   1 tablespoon Chinese rice wine or sake
   1 tablespoon sugar
   pinch of salt
   dash of MSG (optional)

Method:

1. Discard any soft shell from crab meat.

2. Cut bean curd into 1½-inch (6 cm) squares
   and ¼ inch (7 mm) thick. Drain.

3. Heat 2 tablespoons oil, stir-fry half of the
   scallions for 15 seconds, add bean curd, mixture A and ½ cup stock, cook over low heat
   2 to 3 minutes. Thicken with ½ of the dissolved cornstarch and transfer to a serving
   plate.

4. Heat the remaining oil, first stir-fry ginger and
   remaining scallion for 15 seconds, then add
   crab meat and stir-fry for 20 seconds. Add
   pinch of salt, ¼ cup stock and thicken with
   ½ of the dissolved cornstarch. Pour over bean
   curd and serve.

Stir-fried Clams with Bean Curd

蚌肉豆腐
(Pan-jou-tou-fu)   Shanghai

Ingredients:

1 square bean curd, 3″ × 3″ (7.5 × 7.5 cm)

¼ (100 g) clam meat

2–3 tablespoons oil

1 tablespoon minced scallions (substituted for garlic leaves)

1 teaspoon minced fresh ginger

½ tablespoon cornstarch dissolved in 1 tablespoon water

extra pinch of minced scallion for garnishing

Mixture A:

   1 tablespoon Chinese rice wine or sake

   1½ teaspoons sugar

1 tablespoon soy sauce

dash of MSG (optional)

¼ cup chicken stock

Method:

1. Dice bean curd and drain.

2. Wash clams in salted water and drain.

3. Heat oil, stir-fry scallions and ginger for 30 seconds. Add clams, mixture A and bean curd, cover and simmer 3 to 4 minutes. Thicken with dissolved cornstarch and sprinkle chopped scallion on top.

Stir-fried Eels

干煸鳝魚

(Kan-pien-shan-yü)　Chungking

Ingredients:

1 1b. (500 g) sea eels
¼ lb. (100 g) celery
1 scallion, cut into 1⅓-inch (4 cm) sections
1 slice fresh ginger, slivered
1 clove garlic, thinly sliced
2–3 tablespoons oil
1 teaspoon vinegar,
dash of Szechuan peppercorn powder
Mixture A:
　1 tablespoon Chinese rice wine or sake
　2½ tablespoons soy sauce
　1 tablespoon sugar
　1 tablespoon brown bean paste *(tou-pan-chiang*, page 11)

Method:

1. Split and butterfly eels lengthwise, remove heads and bones. Rinse and cut crosswise into 2-inch (6 cm) sections.

2. Cut celery into slivers, about 1⅓ inches (4 cm) long.

3. Heat oil, stir-fry eels until almost done, add mixture A, celery, ginger, garlic, vinegar and 1 tablespoon water, blend thoroughly.

Stir-fried Kelp

脆爆海带

(Tsui-pao-hai-tai)　Hangchow

Ingredients:

2 oz. (50 g) kelp
1 clove garlic, minced
¼ cup flour
oil for deep-frying
1 teaspoon cornstarch　dissolved in ½ tablespoon water
few drops sesame oil
Mixture A:
　1 tablespoon soy sauce
　1 tablespoon Chinese rice wine or sake
　2 tablespoons vinegar
　2 tablespoons sugar
　½ teaspoon salt
　dash of MSG (optional)

Method:

1. Rinse kelp and cut diagonally into diamond shape, about 2 inches (6 cm) wide and 3 inches (9 cm) long. Wipe dry.

2. Mix flour with water to make a smooth batter.

3. Coat kelp with batter and deep-fry over low heat until crisp. Increase heat toward the end of frying and brown the kelp. Drain and set aside.

4. Empty all the oil from pan, bring mixture A and garlic to a boil and thicken with dissolved cornstarch. Drop in fried kelp and blend thoroughly, then sprinkle sesame oil on top and serve.

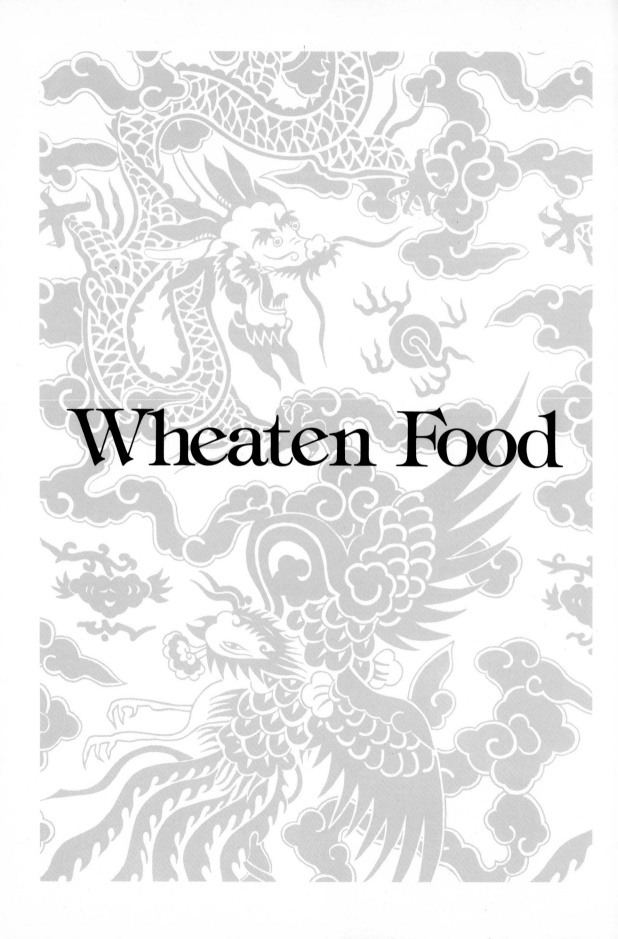

Wheaten Food

Fried Bread

油 餅
(Yu-ping) Peking

Ingredients:

1 lb. (500 g) all-purpose flour
3 teaspoons salt
1 tablespoon baking powder
extra flour for dusting
oil for deep-frying

Method:

1. Combine flour, salt and baking powder. Gradually mix in 2 cups (350 cc) water, ⅓ at a time. Then knead the dough in the bowl to form into 1 piece. Cover, and let stand 15 minutes for the flour to absorb the water.

2. Wet hands with a little water and knead dough again until it becomes smooth. Wrap with damp cloth and let stand for 2 hours.

3. Dust a board with flour. With a rolling pin, roll the entire piece of dough into a flat sheet, about ½ inch (1.5 cm) thick. Cut the sheet into pieces 7 inches (21 cm) long and 5 inches (12.5 cm) wide. Score the surface crosswise by making 2 cuts, ¼ inch (1 cm) deep.

4. Deep-fry until light brown.

Note: Fried dough is served in place of rice with stir-fried vegetables and meat dishes.

Deep-fried Crullers

油条
(Yu-ping) Peking

Ingredients:
1 lb. (500 g) high gluten flour
3 teaspoons salt
1 tablespoon baking powder
extra flour for dusting
oil for deep-frying

Method:
1. Sift flour, salt and baking powder into a bowl and follow the same procedure as step 1 and 2 in Fried Bread.

2. Dust a board with flour, transfer dough onto board and push the dough back and forth to shape into a long ribbon about 2 inches (6 cm) wide and ½ inch (1.5 cm) thick. Cut crosswise into 2-oz. (50 g) strips.

3. Place one strip of dough on top of another and press down with a rolling pin or the blunt side of a cleaver to make them stick together. Pick up two ends and pull to stretch the dough into a thin strip, drop into hot oil and deep-fry until golden brown. Turn the dough while deep-frying. Remove from oil and drain.

Note: Deep-fried crullers are served with rice congee or torn into small chunks and mixed with soup.

Sesame Seed Rolls

糖火燒

(T'ang-huo-shao) Peking

Ingredients:

1½ teaspoons dried yeast
½ teaspoon sugar
14 oz. (400 g) flour
extra flour for dusting
Mixture A:
   3 oz. (75 g) sesame paste (*chih-ma-chiang*,
     page 14)
   3 oz. (75 g) dark brown sugar
   1 tablespoon oil

Method:

1. Sprinkle yeast into 4 tablespoons lukewarm
   water, add sugar and let stand for 5 minutes,
   allow mixture to ferment.

2. Place flour in a bowl, gradually, ⅓ at a time,
   mix in 1 cup of water then the yeast mixture.
   Knead with hands until a dough is formed.
   Let stand 30 minutes.

3. In a small bowl blend mixture A.

4. Divide dough into 3 portions, dust a board
   with flour, and roll each portion into a thin
   rectangular sheet.

5. Spread each sheet with mixture A. Roll up
   the dough and cut crosswise into ½ inch (1.5
   cm) slices. Piece by piece flatten each one with
   the palm to bring the spread and dough together.

6. Brush both sides with oil and fry over low heat
   until slightly brown on both sides. Then bake
   in a medium hot oven 4 to 5 minutes.

Note: Sugar is added to the yeast to help fermenta-
tion. After 5 minutes, if the mixture does not activate,
then the yeast is either too old or has been killed by
the temperature of the water.

    Be sure not to scorch the bread while frying.
Wipe the skillet before cooking each new batch.

Fried Sesame Biscuit

燒 餅
(Shao-ping)　Peking

Ingredients:
1½ teaspoons dried yeast
½ teaspoon sugar
1 teaspoon Szechuan peppercorns
1 teaspoon fennel seeds
½ teaspoon salt
2 oz. (50 g) sesame paste (*chih-ma-chang*,
　page 14)
2 oz. (50 g) sugar
2 tablespoons toasted white sesame seeds

Method:
1. Sprinkle yeast into 4 tablespoons lukewarm water, add ½ teaspoon sugar and let stand 5 minutes.

2. First mix flour with 1 cup water, then blend in the yeast mixture and mix thoroughly by hand. Let stand ½ hour to 1 hour.

3. In a heavy pan, toast Szechuan peppercorns, fennel seeds and salt togehter over low heat for 3 minutes, then pulverize. Mix sesame paste with the spices.

4. Divide dough into 2 portions, dust a board with flour, and roll each piece into a thin rectangular sheet.

5. Spread each sheet with ½ of the sesame paste mixture, roll up the dough and cut crosswise 1-inch (3 cm) pieces. Press the dough with fingers and stretch into a biscuit about 2 inches (6 cm) in diameter.

6. Caramel remaining 2 oz. (50 g) sugar with little water.

7. Brush both sides of each biscuit with caramel and sprinkle with sesame seeds.

8. Brown biscuits slightly in a skillet, then bake in a medium hot oven for 4 to 5 minutes.

Note: The picture shows what the biscuits look like after being pressed and stretched with fingers.

Chinese Biscuit

酥 火 燒
(*Su-huo-shao*)　Peking

Ingredients:

Mixture A:
   14 oz. (375 g) flour
   1½ teaspoons salt
   1 cup water

Mixture B:
   5 oz. (125 g) flour
   ⅓ cup oil

Method:

1. Mix mixture A and knead until smooth. Let stand for 10 minutes.

2. Heat ⅓ cup oil in mixture B until hot then blend in flour and knead until smooth. Let stand for 10 minutes.

3. On a floured surface, roll out mixture A and mixture B separately into 2 rectangular pieces of the same size.

4. Place B dough on top of A dough and roll them together into a long cylinder. Cut the cylinder crosswise into pieces about 1 inch (3 cm) thick. Press and flatten each piece to ½ inch (1.5 cm) thick. Oil both sides, then brown in a skillet. Place the browned pieces on a baking sheet, and bake for 4 to 5 minutes.

Note: One tablespoon sugar may be added to Mixture B.

The term "*su*" in the title refers to crisply baked doughs.

Chinese Meat Buns

包子
(Pao-tzŭ) Peking

Ingredients:
3 teaspoons dried yeast
1 teaspoon sugar
1 lb. (500 g) flour
extra flour for dusting
Mixture A:
   ½ lb. (250 g) ground pork
   2 tablespoons minced scallions
   1 teaspoon minced fresh ginger
   4½ tablespoons soy sauce
   2 tablespoons oil

Method:
1. Sprinkle dried yeast into 5 tablespoons luke-warm water and add sugar. Let stand for 5 minutes.

2. Place flour in a large bowl. Mix in 1⅓ cups water gradually, about ⅓ of amount at one time, then stir in the yeast mixture. Knead until a smooth dough is formed. Cover and let stand for 1 hour.

3. Combine mixture A and stir in ½ cup water, mix thoroughly.

4. When dough becomes double in size, roll and push dough on a floured surface back and forth with both hands to make a long cylinder about 1⅓ inches (4 cm) in diameter. Cut the cylinder into 25 to 30 sections. With the cut side facing up, flatten each section with hand into a round wrapping about 2½ inches (8 cm) in diameter.

5. Place 1 tablespoon filling in the center of each wrapping. Gather the edges and pinch them together tightly at the top by making a few pleats.

6. Oil the steamer tray, place buns in the tray leaving enough space between them. Steam over high heat for 6 to 7 minutes.

Note: The buns in the recipe are quite small. To make sweet buns, simply replace the meat filling with Chinese sweet red bean paste.

Menu A
Fried Chicken with Bamboo Shoots
Stir-fried Green Peppers
Bean Curd Soup with Mushrooms and Bamboo Shoots

Menu B
Celery Salad
Braised Chicken with Potatoes
Clear Fish Soup

Menu C
Sweet-and-Sour Pork
Stir-fried Bean Curd with Preserved Cucumbers
Stir-fried String Beans
Giant White Radish and Shrimp Soup

Menu D
Carrot Salad
Stir-fried Kelp
Braised Chicken
Fillet of Fish with Wine Sauce
Pearl Balls
Fish Ball Soup

Menu E
Boiled Shrimp
Cucumber Salad
Sweet-and-Sour Carp
Braised Pork with Chestnuts
Crab Meat with Bean Curd
Steamed Chicken

Menu F
Tomatoes with Meat Sauce
Shrimp and Deep-fried Bean Curd Soup
Egg with Crab Meat
Chinese Meat Buns

Menu A

Fried Chicken with Bamboo
  Shoots, page 91
Stir-fried Green Peppers,
  page 28
Bean Curd Soup with Mush-
  rooms and Bamboo
  Shoots, page 42

Menu D

Menu E

Boiled Shrimp, page 108
Cucumber Salad, page 21
Sweet-and-Sour Carp,
  page 94
Braised Pork with Chestnuts,
  page 62
Crab Meat with Bean Curd,
  page 109
Steamed Chicken in a Bowl,
  page 91

Menu F

Cuts of Pork

Pork is the predominant meat in Chinese cooking. Of the 97 meat recipes in "The Masses Cookbook" only 4 are beef and 2 are lamb dishes, the rest are all dishes of pork or pork parts. In order to create delicious Chinese food, one must choose the correct cut of meat for each individual dish. The more frequently used cuts of pork are tenderloin, loin, fresh ham and spareribs. There were many dishes in the book calling for boneless spareribs or belly pork; this cut usually consists of much fat. If fat meat is not part of one's dietary habits, substitute a leaner cut such as fresh ham, or any other cut according to preference.

Belly pork with layers of alternating lean and fat meat is called *Wu-hua-chu-jou* 五花猪肉 (Five-flower-pork), this cut is used for pork stew. Loin and fresh ham are good for stir-fying and spareribs for simmering.

The meat of high quality pork must be light pink and firm. The grain of the meat should be thick and resilient. Pork spoils quicker than beef, buy the freshest possible and use promptly

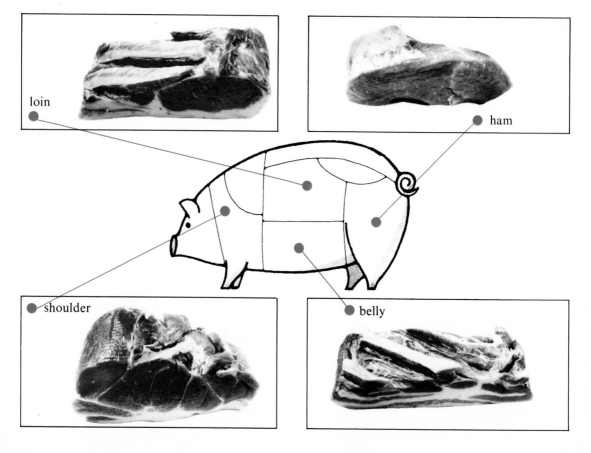

loin

ham

shoulder

belly

How to Prepare Chicken

In many Chinese dishes the chicken is cooked whole. When a small amount is needed, the chicken is cut up and used for different dishes which require certain cuts of the fowl. When carving a whole cooked chicken, the pieces should be cut approximately the same size. Chicken cooked with the bones attached will have a more texture and a richer taste. For stir-frying dishes, however boneless chicken is preferable. Boned chicken breast, legs and thighs are better for quick stir-fried dishes than other parts.

Chicken is cut up and divided as shown in the drawing. The thin fillet along the ribs is excellent food for old people, because it is tender and free of fat. Bones and skins should be used for soup stock.

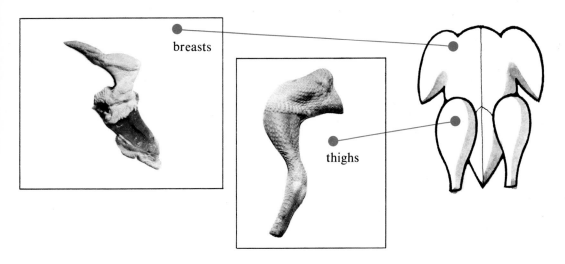

breasts

thighs

How to Make Chicken Stock

Making soups or sauces with chicken stock instead of water enhances the taste of the dish. Liquid used for boiling meat or soaking dried shrimp should be saved for the stock pot. When in a hurry bouillon cubes dissolved in water make a good substitute. When bouillon cubes are used the amount of salt in the dish should be reduced.

Chicken stock can be made as follows:

In a heavy kettle, bring to a boil 10 to 12 cups water, chicken and/or chicken bones, 1 scallion, 2 slices fresh ginger, 1 tablespoon rice wine and 1 chicken bouillon cube. Remove any scum, reduce heat and simmer uncovered for 1 hour. Discard bones and strain stock immediately. Reserve chicken meat for salad. Pork or pork bones or fish bones can also be used for making but chicken stock is most flavorful and is simpler to prepare.

Index

135